M000282691

A
Golden
Treasury
of
Puritan
Devotion

A
Golden
Treasury
of
Puritan
Devotion

*Selections from
the Writings of
Thirteen Puritan Divines*

Compiled and Edited by
Mariano Di Gangi

P&R
PUBLISHING
P.O. BOX 817 • PHILLIPSBURG • NEW JERSEY 08865-0817

© 1999 by Mariano Di Gangi

All rights reserved. No part of this book may be reproduced, stored in a retrieval system, or transmitted in any form or by any means—electronic, mechanical, photocopy, recording, or otherwise—except for brief quotations for the purpose of review or comment, without the prior permission of the publisher, P&R Publishing Company, P.O. Box 817, Phillipsburg, New Jersey 08865-0817.

Page design by Tobias Design
Typesetting by Michelle Feaster

Printed in the United States of America

Library of Congress Cataloging-in-Publication Data

A golden treasury of Puritan devotion : selections from the writings of thirteen Puritan divines / compiled and edited by Mariano Di Gangi.
    p.   cm.
  Includes bibliographical references.
  ISBN 0-87552-173-8 (pbk.)
  1. Devotional literature, English. 2. Puritans. I. Di Gangi, Mariano.
  BX9322 .G65 1999
  242—dc21   98-35649

To my wife,

Ninette,

with gratitude for
over fifty years together
in the new life of God's grace

"Marriage is a most honourable thing . . . instituted by God in
paradise, ordained so that man and wife might be a mutual help to one
another in adversity and prosperity, in sickness and in health . . .
Great is the mystery set forth by marriage—the sacred, spiritual, real,
and inviolable union betwixt Christ and His Church."

— William Gouge, 1626.

❧ CONTENTS ❧

❧ INTRODUCTION ❧

The Puritans of the seventeenth century are often caricatured as gloomy fanatics, rigid sectarians, pre-Victorian prudes, and downright killjoys, dedicated to the ponderous presentation and imperious imposition of a narrow-minded morality from pulpits standing six feet above contradiction. They are accused of disliking the "sport" of bear-baiting, not because it brought pain to the bear but because it gave pleasure to the spectators. According to one historian who should have known better, "The extreme Puritan was at once recognised by his gait, his garb, his lank hair, the sour solemnity of his face, the upturned white of his eyes, the nasal twang with which he spoke, and, above all, by his peculiar dialect . . . the imagery and style of Scripture" provoking "the derision of both prelatists and libertines."[1]

It is, of course, unfair to blame everything that is perceived as repressive in Protestant culture on the Puritans. They were not killjoys or prudes. "They dressed as befitted their social class, participated in lotteries, drank alcoholic beverages, and approached sex as more than a mere obligation."[2] What the Puritans condemned, however, was drunkenness and extramarital sex. They also had a high sense of stewardship, which shaped their work ethic. "The ideal of Puritan moral life was one of sober moderation."[3]

Ridiculed as incurable pessimists whose obsession with sin drove them to morbid introspection and destructive despair, the Puritans were in reality skilled physicians and surgeons of the soul, who presented and applied the Good News of God's redeeming grace to all who would turn to Christ for salvation. They not only denounced the sin that occasioned corruption and condemnation, but announced the forgiveness of sins and a new life in fellowship with God.

1

The Puritans were "a breed of giants" characterized by "mature holiness and seasoned fortitude."[4] Their focus was on pastoral care for persons in need: "the analysis of cases of conscience, the resolution of doubts, and helping people who were in trouble."[5]

They were not all of one mind on everything. The Puritans had their differences on the relationship between church and state. They held a variety of views regarding church government: Episcopal, Presbyterian, and congregational/independent. They differed on the mode and subjects of baptism. But they were all trinitarians who received the Scriptures as divinely inspired, and therefore authoritative for both creed and conduct. They accepted the doctrine of the sovereignty of God, along with predestination and election. They also emphasized the necessity of regeneration and called the penitent to put their trust in Christ for salvation. An admirable balance is evident in Puritanism at its best: the redemptive work of Christ *for* us, and the renovating ministry of His Spirit *in* us.

Puritan preachers proclaimed the gospel doctrine of justification—absolution, acquittal, and acceptance by a holy God—through faith in Jesus Christ. They also called believers to a new life of holiness—the experience of sanctification—resulting in likeness to Christ. "Puritanism was at heart a spiritual movement, passionately concerned with God and godliness . . . a movement for church reform, pastoral renewal, evangelism, and spiritual revival."[6]

Puritan pastors were exemplary educators. Starting with a text from Scripture, they usually analyzed it into various heads of doctrine. That analysis would be followed by corroboration from other biblical passages, and clarification to avoid any misunderstandings. Objections would then be answered. Analogies would help to illustrate the truth expounded. But no sermon would be complete without a full presentation of "uses." Puritan preaching was not a theoretical exercise majoring in pale abstractions. It aimed at giving people a gospel that not only made sense, but would also make a difference. The application of the truth was to result in holiness of life.

The Puritans lived and labored in turbulent times, in no small measure agitated by conflict over the direction and pace of change in the Church of England. Some looked longingly back to Rome, others gravitated toward Geneva, and still others stood for the status quo. Should nonconformity be permitted regarding ritual and vestments where there is no clear biblical mandate? Or, should uniformity be obligatory, with severe penalties for noncompliance? Should one work for reform generally from within the national church, or withdraw and affiliate with another group? These issues are still with us today.

To understand some of the tensions and troubles of the Puritan era, one has to go back at least as far as Henry VIII. He had no real interest in furthering the Reformation. His main preoccupations seem to have been the production of a male heir to the throne, plundering monasteries, and incorporating some papal pretensions into his royal job description. Henry's son, Edward VI, was godly but sickly. He was definitely committed to the Christ of the Gospels and the reform of the church but died in 1553 at the young age of sixteen. Then came Mary Tudor, whose reign was marked by the exile or execution of more than a few Protestant leaders. She was succeeded by Elizabeth I, who secured the establishment of the Church of England. When she died in 1603, her cousin became king of England and Scotland as James I.

During the reign of James I, internal conflicts intensified. As Puritanism progressed, presbyterial and congregational forms of church government were seen as alternatives to an enforced episcopacy. There was also a growing debate over conformity to doctrines and practices that seemed to lack a clear scriptural mandate. Charles I, son of James I, firmly believed in the divine right of kings. His demands for money ran into strong parliamentary resistance. Gridlock led to the dissolution of Parliament, which did not sit from 1629 to 1640. The struggle for political supremacy persisted. Dissenters were persecuted as the king and his high church allies pushed for Arminian theology and the restoration of Romanist ritual. Civil war broke out in 1642, and the king's forces were defeated by Oliver Cromwell's New Model Army. Meanwhile, the

Westminster Assembly of Divines began its work. Between 1643 and 1649, it would produce the Confession of Faith and its Larger and Shorter Catechisms.

King Charles I was imprisoned, condemned, and then executed in January 1649. All did not go well, however, in Cromwell's Commonwealth. The victors let their differences divide them. With Cromwell's death in 1658, the way was open for Charles II in the spring of 1660. Soon, the rigorous enforcement of the Act of Uniformity would compel many men of conscience to face expulsion from their parishes and ejection from their pulpits. About two thousand pastors were thus deprived. Nevertheless, Puritans within and without the national church continued to preach "the experience of grace in the lives of believers . . . justification by faith, and the experience of regeneration and progressive sanctification."[7]

Some of the issues the Puritans faced were not altogether different from those we encounter today. What was once a conflict between king and pope became a struggle between king and Parliament, and now is a battle between the executive and legislative branches of government. The situation is complicated by the tendency of courts to legislate via decisions in some controversial cases. The outbreak of civil war over political and religious considerations should not surprise us. Supposedly civilized peoples still engage in atrocities as they pursue "ethnic cleansing." Racism, like greed, is still a curse.

The Puritans denounced such sins as swearing, drunkenness, murder, adultery, and Sabbath-breaking. We have seen sin abound, with clerics who cannot keep their hands off women and their fingers out of the till. Pregnancy is now considered a sexually transmitted disease curable by abortion. Gambling is encouraged by the state, doctor-assisted suicide finds increasing acceptance, and same-sex relationships are no longer a barrier to ordination in some quarters. Like the Puritans, we need to emphasize the practical uses of God's moral law as well as proclaim His redeeming love. Justification divorced from sanctification will never lead to glorification.

Puritan publications often bear titles as complex as they are quaint. Consider that of William Gurnall's classic on spiritual conflict:

The Christian in Complete Armour;
A Treatise
Of the Saints' War Against the Devil:

Wherein a discovery is made of that grand Enemy
of God and his People, in his Policies,
Power, Seat of his Empire, Wickedness,
and chief design he hath against the Saints.

A Magazine Opened,
From whence the Christian is furnished with Spiritual
Arms for the Battle, helped on with his Armour,
and taught the use of his Weapon: together
with the happy issue of the whole War.

There can be no doubt, however, about the seriousness of Puritan preachers in expounding and applying the whole counsel of God—precepts as well as promises and prophecies, doctrines and duties no less than the divided destinies of the believing and impenitent.

This modest anthology includes over five hundred quotations gleaned from several thousand pages written by thirteen Puritan authors: Stephen Charnock, Robert Leighton, Richard Sibbes, Thomas Watson, John Owen, William Gouge, Henry Smith, John Bunyan, William Gurnall, John Howe, Thomas Manton, Richard Baxter, and James Janeway. Time and space would fail me to tell of John Flavel, Thomas Brooks, William Ames, Thomas Goodwin, William Perkins, and others who through faith confronted kings, challenged oppression, endured exile, suffered imprisonment, and proved equally valiant for truth.

Life, liberty, and the pursuit of happiness are considered by many to be their inalienable rights from the hand of some distant deity. But life is blighted by moral failure, freedom becomes rebellion and ends in anarchy, and the hedonistic pursuit of happiness has displaced the quest for godliness. The Puritans, with their intense focus on the majesty, might, and mercy of the Lord, can help us rediscover the truths we must apply to our lives. Let us learn from them just what it means to glorify God, and find lasting pleasure in the process.

Acknowledgments

My thanks are due to Miss Cathy Knox for her assistance in the preparation of the typescript for publication.

In this sampling of Puritan devotion, comparatively few words and phrases have been updated. Occasional connectives, to maintain continuity between quotations, are enclosed in brackets.

The portraits of Richard Baxter, Stephen Charnock, John Howe, and John Owen are engravings printed in Daniel Neal, *The History of the Puritans or Protestant Nonconformists*, 2 vols. (New York: Harper and Brothers, 1843).

Quotations from *A Quest for Godliness: The Puritan Vision of the Christian Life*, James I. Packer, © 1990, are used by permission of Good News Publishers/Crossway Books, Wheaton, Ill. 60187.

ONE

❧ STEPHEN CHARNOCK ❧

1 6 2 8 – 8 0

After studies at Cambridge, where he had a conversion experience, Stephen Charnock went on to teach at New College, Oxford. There he attended a church pastored by the renowned Thomas Goodwin.

Charnock became chaplain to Henry Cromwell (son of Oliver) in 1655 and had a fruitful ministry in Ireland until the Act of Uniformity was passed five years later. Returning to England, he served as joint pastor with Thomas Watson at Crosby Hall in London. Using a magnifying glass and a laboured delivery that was frequently flat, requiring careful attention from his hearers, Charnock was not a popular pulpiteer. He was considered a preacher's preacher, devoted to dealing with weighty themes. His masterpiece on The Existence and Attributes of God, *published posthumously in 1681, has since been reprinted numerous times.*

The Existence and Attributes of God

The fool, one that has lost his wisdom and right notion of God and divine things, which were communicated to many by creation, has said in his heart: "There is no God." He is dead in sin, yet not so much void of rational faculties as of grace in these faculties; not one who lacks reason, but abuses his reason . . . It is a great folly to deny or doubt of the existence or being of God.[1]

A secret atheism, or a partial atheism, is the spring of all the wicked practices in the world; the disorders of life spring from the ill dispositions of the heart.

The world [once] ran from one God to many, and our age is running from one God to none at all.[2]

He who seeks after God according to the mind of God must believe that he is such a God that will pardon sin and justify a seeker of him . . . No man can seek God, or love God, unless he believe him to be thus.

It is folly to deny or doubt of a sovereign being, incomprehensible in his nature, infinite in his essence and perfections, independent in his operations, who has given being to the whole frame of sensible and intelligible creatures, and governs them according to their several natures by an unconceivable wisdom, who fills the heavens with the glory of his majesty, and the earth with the influences of his goodness.[3]

If it be folly to deny the being of God, it will be our wisdom, since we acknowledge his being, to think of him often.[4]

We have had no settled abode in the earth since the time of Abraham's being called out from Ur of the Chaldees. We have had Canaan in a promise, we have it not yet in possession; we have been exposed to the cruelties of an oppressing enemy, and the inconveniences of a desert wilderness . . . You have been our shield against dangers, our security in times of trouble . . . You have been our dwelling place; you have kept open-house for us, sheltered us against storms, and preserved us from mischief . . . in all generations . . . Our refuge and defense have not been from created things; not from the ark, but from the God of the ark . . . He is a dwelling place to secure his people here, or entertain them above.[5]

Though we cannot comprehend eternity, yet we may comprehend that there is an eternity . . . a perpetual duration, which has neither beginning nor end. Time has both.

God is eternal, we exclude from him all possibility of beginning and ending, all flux and change . . . His duration is as endless as his essence is boundless . . . this is an excellency belonging to the Supreme Being.[6]

If God be of an eternal duration, then Christ is God. Eternity is the property of God, yet is ascribed to Christ (Col. 1:17) . . . He is the same, yesterday, today, and for ever (Heb. 13:8).

The gospel is not preached by the command of a new and temporary God, but of that God who was before all ages.[7]

Since God can only rejoice in goodness, the creatures must have that goodness restored to them which they had at the first creation . . . The goodness of the creatures is the glory and joy of God. We may infer from this what a base and vile thing sin is, which lays the foundation of the world's change. Sin brings it to decrepit age. Sin overturned the whole work of God . . . Let us look upon sin with no other notion than as the object of God's hatred, the cause of his grief in the creatures, and the spring of the pain and ruin of the world.

God, as immutable, is contrasted with all creatures as perishing and changeable. He is unchangeable in his essence, nature, and perfections.[8]

God is unchangeable with regard to his will and purpose . . . Whatsoever God has decreed, is immutable; whatsoever God has promised, shall be accomplished . . . He is the Lord Jehovah, therefore he is true to his word (Mal. 3:6; Isa. 43:13) . . . Where we find predictions in Scripture declared and yet not executed, we must consider them not as absolute, but conditional . . . So Nineveh shall be destroyed . . . unless the inhabitants repent, which they did.[9]

What comfort would it be to pray to a God that, like the chameleon, changed colours every day, every moment?[10]

The immutability of God is a strong ground of consolation . . . and encourages hope and confidence.[11]

While we have him for our God, we have his immutability, as well as any other perfection of his nature, for our advantage. The nearer we come to him, the more stability we shall have in ourselves; the further from him, the more liable to change . . . Let us also desire those things which are nearest to him in this perfection: the righteousness of Christ, that shall never wear out; and the grace of the Spirit, that shall never burn out. By this means, what God is infinitely by nature, we shall come to be finitely, immutable by grace, as much as the capacity of a creature can obtain.[12]

As eternity is the perfection whereby he has neither beginning nor end, immutability is the perfection whereby he has neither increase nor diminution, so immensity or omnipresence is that whereby he has neither bounds nor limitation . . . As he is not measured by time, so he is not limited by place . . . His nature has no bounds; he is not tied to any place as the creature is, who, when he is present in one place, is absent from another. As no place can be without God, so no place can compass and contain him . . . He has a presence of glory in heaven, whereby he comforts the saints; a presence of wrath in hell, whereby he torments the damned (Ps. 139:7–9).[13]

How terrible should the thoughts of this attribute [God's omnipresence] be to sinners! How foolish is it to imagine any hiding-place from the incomprehensible God who is present in every point of the world.

That God is present everywhere, is as much a comfort to a good man as it is a terror to a wicked one. He is everywhere for his people . . . by an immense diffusion of his goodness . . . The omnipresence of God is comfort in all violent temptations [and] sharp afflictions—a spur to holy actions . . . Communion with God consists chiefly in an ordering of our ways as in the presence of him who is invisible . . . Let it therefore be our desire that as he fills heaven and earth by his essence, he may fill our understandings and wills by his grace.[14]

"Great is our Lord, and of great power: his understanding is infinite" (Ps. 148:5). As God is almighty, so he is omniscient . . . If men thought they had to deal with an ignorant Deity, there could be no bar to the worst of crimes [and] no practice of religion.[15]

The knowledge of God has respect to things present, past, future . . . He knows all creatures, from the highest to the least as well as the greatest . . . God knows all the actions of creatures [and] all their thoughts . . . God descends into the depths and abysses of the soul, discerns the most inward contrivances; nothing is impenetrable to him (Heb. 4:12f.) . . . God discerns all good motions of the mind and will [as well as] all the evils and sins of creatures.[16]

The whole prophetic part of Scripture declares this perfection of God. Every prophetic candle was lighted at this torch; they could not have had this foreknowledge of themselves . . . The subjects of prophecy are things future, and no man is properly a prophet but in prediction.[17]

God foreknows all things, as present with him from eternity . . . All things are present to God's knowledge, though in their own nature they may be past or future.[18]

God foreknows the voluntary sinful motions of men's wills. Were not all the minute sinful circumstances about the death of our blessed Redeemer, as the piercing of him, giving him gall to drink, foretold? What were those but the free actions of men, which they did willingly, without any constraint?[19]

But what if the foreknowledge of God, and the liberty of the will, cannot be fully reconciled by man? Shall we therefore deny a perfection in God to support a liberty in ourselves? Shall we rather fasten ignorance upon God, and accuse him of blindness, to maintain our liberty? That God foreknows everything, and yet there is liberty in the rational creature, are both certain, but how fully to reconcile them may surmount the understanding of man.[20]

God knows all things infallibly. His understanding is infinite in regard of certainty . . . Since he is essentially omniscient, he is no more capable of error in his understanding, than of imperfection in his essence; his counsels are as unerring as his essence is perfect.[21]

If God were not omniscient, how could he reward the good, and punish the evil? The works of men are either rewardable or punishable, not according to their outward circumstances, but inward principles and ends, and the degrees of venom lurking in the heart. The exact discerning of these . . . is necessary to pass a right and infallible judgment upon them . . . Without such a knowledge and discerning, men would not have their due . . . It is necessary therefore that the supreme Judge of the world should not be thought to be blindfolded when he distributes his rewards and punishments, and muffle his face when he passes his sentence . . . This is the glory of God, to discover the secret of all hearts at last (I Cor. 4:5).[22]

This perfection of God [omniscience] fits him to be a special object of trust. If he were forgetful, what comfort could we have in any promise? How could we depend upon him if he were ignorant of our state? His compassion to pity us, his readiness to revive us, his power to protect and assist us, would be insignificant without his omniscience to inform his goodness and direct the arm of his power. This perfection is, as it were, God's office of intelligence . . . You may depend upon his mercy that has promised, and upon his truth to perform, upon his sufficiency to supply and his goodness to relieve, and his righteousness to reward you, because he has an infinite understanding of you and your needs.[23]

All truth is to be drawn from Scripture . . . the source of divine knowledge; not the traditions of men, nor reason separate from Scripture. Whosoever brings another doctrine coins another Christ. Nothing is to be added to what is written, nothing detracted from it. He does not send us for truth to the puddles of human inventions, to the enthusiasms of our brain, nor to the see of Rome, no, nor to the instruction of angels, but the writings of the prophets, as they clear up the declarations of the apostles.[24]

The wisdom of God appears in creation, in the government of his creatures, and the redemption of man . . . Study and admire the wisdom of God . . . this is the duty of all Christians.[25]

We cannot have a conception of God, if we conceive him not most powerful, as well as most wise. He is not a God who cannot do what he will, and perform all his pleasure. If we imagine him restrained in his power, we imagine him limited in his essence. As he has an infinite knowledge to know what is possible, he cannot be without an infinite power to do what is possible. As he has a will to resolve what he sees good, so he cannot lack a power to effect what he sees good to decree . . . You cannot conceive an infinite essence without an infinite power of activity . . . We must imagine him to be of an infinite power and strength.[26]

The power of God is that ability and strength whereby he can bring to pass whatsoever he please, whatsoever his infinite wisdom can direct, and whatsoever the infinite purity of his will can resolve.[27]

Some things are impossible to the nature and being of God . . . He cannot die who is life itself . . . God cannot do anything unbecoming his holiness and goodness . . . any unrighteous thing. God cannot love sin . . . The will of God cannot will anything but what is worthy of him . . . It is impossible for God to lie (Heb. 6:13); God cannot deny himself (II Tim. 2:13), because of his faithfulness . . . God is omnipotent, because he cannot do evil, and would not be omnipotent if he could.[28]

The power of God appears in creation . . . By this creative power God is often distinguished from all the idols and false gods in the world . . . As there was need of his power to execute his decree of creation, there is also need of his power to execute his decree about the matter of government: a natural providence, which consists in the preservation and propagation of all things; a moral government [relating to] the hearts and actions of men; a gracious government, as respecting the Church.[29]

The divine power in temporal deliverances and freedom from the slavery of human oppressors prefigures that which glitters in redemption, whereby the devil is defeated in his designs, stripped of his spoils, and yoked in his strength.[30]

Holiness is a glorious perfection belonging to the nature of God, hence he is in Scripture styled often the Holy One . . . This is his greatest title of honour; in this does the majesty and venerableness of his name appear (Ex. 15:11; Isa. 42:21) . . . Power is his hand and arm, omniscience his eye, mercy his viscera, eternity his duration, holiness his beauty.[31]

The holiness of God *negatively* is a perfect freedom from all evil . . . estranged from all shadow of evil, of all imaginable contagion. *Positively,* it is the rectitude or integrity of the divine nature . . . that conformity in affection and action to the divine will as to his eternal law, whereby he works with a becomingness to his own excellency, and has a delight and complacency in everything agreeable to his will, and an abhorrence of everything contrary to it.[32]

His holiness appears as he is creator, in framing man in a perfect uprightness . . . His holiness appears in his laws, as he is a lawgiver and a judge . . . His holiness appears in the allurements annexed to the law for keeping it, and the affrightments to restrain from the breaking of it . . . His holiness appears in the judgments inflicted for the violation of this law. Divine holiness is the root of divine justice and divine justice is the triumph of divine holiness.[33]

Christ suffered himself to be pierced to death, that sin—the enemy of God's purity—might be destroyed, and the honour of the law—the image of God's holiness—might be repaired and fulfilled in the fallen creature.[34]

If holiness be an eminent perfection of divine nature, the Christian religion is of a divine extraction. It discovers the holiness of God, and forms the creature to a conformity to him . . . This attribute frowns upon fallen nature, but smiles on the restorations made by the gospel. God's holiness, in conjunction with his justice, is terrible to a guilty sinner. But now, in conjunction with his mercy, by the satisfaction of Christ, it is sweet to a believing penitent.[35]

Without a due sense of it [the holiness of God], we can never exalt God in our hearts; and the more distinct conceptions we have of this and the rest of his attributes, the more we glorify him . . . Deprive not God of the design of his own glory (Lev. 10:3).[36]

God alone is infinitely good. A boundless goodness that knows no limits, a goodness as infinite as his essence, not only good but best; not only good, but goodness itself, the supreme unconceivable goodness.[37]

The holiness of God is the rectitude of his nature, whereby he is pure, and without spot in himself. The goodness of God is the efflux of his will, whereby he is beneficial to his creatures.[38]

The severe punishment of offenders, and the afflictions he inflicts upon his servants, are no violations of his goodness. To punish wickedness is right, and therefore good . . . As for afflictions, they are marks of a greater measure of fatherly goodness . . . to correct his child . . . and breed him up to virtue and honour (Heb. 12:6, 7).[39]

The goodness of God appears in the laws he has given to man, engaging him to obedience by promises and threatenings . . . He promises, that he might be a rewarder; and threatens, that he might not be a punisher: the one to elevate our hope, and the other to excite our fear—the two passions whereby the nature of man is managed in the world.[40]

The whole gospel is nothing but one entire mirror of divine goodness. The whole of redemption is wrapped up in that one expression of the angels' song, "Good will towards men" (Luke 2:14) . . . Goodness was the spring of redemption . . . He was under no obligation to pity our misery and repair our ruins . . . There was no goodness in us to be the motive of his love, but his goodness was the fountain of our benefit (John 3:16).[41]

God's first resolution to redeem, and the means appointed for redemption, could have no other inducement but divine goodness . . . God sent his Son (John 3:34; 5:24; 17:3). To what end did God send Christ but to redeem?

His intention of saving was before the mission of a Saviour . . . It is true Christ gave himself, but by the order of divine goodness . . . He is therefore called "the Lamb of God" as being set apart by God to be a propitiating and appeasing sacrifice . . . as divine goodness intended for our rescue. In God's giving Christ to be our Redeemer, he gave the highest gift that it was possible for divine goodness to bestow—"the image of his person, and the brightness of his glory" (Heb. 1:3) . . . There is something in Christ more excellent and comely than the office of a saviour; the greatness of his person is more excellent than the salvation procured by his death.[42]

This Son . . . was a gift to us; for our sakes he descended from his throne, and dwelt on earth; for our sakes he was made flesh . . . made a curse, and scorched in the furnace of his Father's wrath . . . He gave him to us, to suffer for us as a man, and redeem us as a God; to be a sacrifice to expiate our sin by translating the punishment upon himself, which was merited by us. Thus was he made low to exalt us, and debased to advance us, made poor to enrich us (II Cor. 8:9) . . . He was ordered to taste the bitter cup of death, that we might drink of the rivers of immortal life . . . Thus was the righteous given for sin, the innocent for criminals, the glory of heaven for the dregs of death, and the immense riches of a Deity expended to restock man.[43]

Such pains does goodness take with men, to make them candidates for heaven. How readily does he receive them when they return . . . A sincere look from the creature draws out his arms, and opens his bosoms . . . He does not only stand ready to receive our petitions while we are speaking, but "answers us before we call" (Isa. 65:24); listening to the motions of our hearts, as well as the supplications of our lips. He is the true Father, who has a quicker pace in meeting, than the prodigal has in returning . . . because "he delights in mercy" (Mic. 7:18); he delights in the expressions of it from himself, and the acceptance of it by his creature.[44]

Divine goodness is eminent in the sacraments he has joined to this [new] covenant, especially in the Lord's Supper. As he gave himself in his Son, so he gives his Son in the sacrament . . . for the expiation of our crimes [and] the nourishment of our souls . . . His goodness is seen in the sacrament, in giving us in it a union and communion with Christ. There is not only a *commemoration* of Christ dying, but a *communication* of Christ living (I Cor. 10:16, 17) . . . How great is this goodness of God![45]

Neglect not this ordinance. If it be a token of divine goodness to appoint it, it is no sign of our estimation of divine goodness to neglect it.[46]

The goodness in redemption extends itself to the lower creation. It takes in not only man, but the whole of creation, except the fallen angels . . . The fall of man brought misery not only upon himself, but a vanity upon the creature; the earth groaned under a curse for his sake . . . debased to serve the lusts of a traitor; his enmity, luxury, sensuality.

But when all the fruits of redemption shall be completed, the goodness of God shall pour itself upon the creatures, "deliver them from the bondage of corruption into the glorious liberty of the children of God" . . . freed from the vanity under which they are enslaved (Rom. 8:21) . . . Nature shall put on triumphant vestments . . . Thus does the divine goodness spread its kind arms over all the whole creation.[47]

If God be so good, how unworthy is the contempt and abuse of his goodness! The contempt and abuse of divine goodness is frequent and common. It began in the first ages of the world, and commenced a few moments after the creation . . . Adam began the dance, and his posterity have followed him.[48]

God takes this contempt of his goodness heinously . . . How is God's goodness abused? By a forgetfulness of his benefits . . . by an impatient murmuring . . . by a distrust of his providence . . . by omissions of duty . . . [and] when we give up our souls and affections to those benefits we have from God, when we make those things his rivals.[49]

All true blessings grow up from the pardon of sin . . . The principal intent of Christ was expiation of sin . . . Where sin is pardoned, the soul is renewed (Ps. 103:3) . . . God is the sole and sovereign author of all spiritual blessings . . . his empire has no vicars-general . . . Since his throne is in the heavens, all things under the heaven are parts of his dominion (Ps. 103:19) . . . He looks down majestically, and by the way of authority, not as a bare spectator, but the look of a governor, to pass sentence upon them as a judge . . . God is sovereign Lord and King . . . He has an absolute authority over the greatest and the least of creatures . . . he is the King of glory, the supreme Monarch.[50]

As God is Lord, he has a right to enact; as he is almighty, he has a power to execute . . . Yet this dominion, though it be absolute, is not tyrannical; but it is managed by the rules of wisdom, righteousness, and goodness.[51]

The Lord God is merciful, gracious, and long-suffering (Ex. 34:6) . . . Patience differs from mercy. Mercy regards the creature as miserable, patience respects the creature as criminal; mercy pities him in his misery, and patience bears with the sin which engendered that misery . . . His patience is manifested to our first parents . . . to the Gentiles . . . to the Israelites . . . He speaks before he strikes.[52]

Let us imitate God's patience in our own to others . . . The consideration of divine patience should make us square ourselves according to that pattern . . . How distant are they from the nature of God, who are in a flame upon every slight provocation . . . As patience is God's perfection, so it is the accomplishment of the soul. And as his slowness to anger argues the greatness of his power over himself, so an unwillingness to revenge is a sign of a power over ourselves; which is more noble than to be a monarch over others.[53]

TWO

❧ ROBERT LEIGHTON ❧

1 6 1 1 — 8 4

Robert Leighton was the son of a Presbyterian manse, ordained by presbytery to the ministry, and signer of the Solemn League and Covenant in 1643. This Puritan expositor of Scripture became principal of the University of Edinburgh, bishop of Dunblane, and afterward archbishop of Glasgow. With the establishment of episcopacy in Scotland, he decided to remain within the Anglican communion. Leighton pleaded with Charles II on behalf of the nonconformists and hoped to secure toleration for Presbyterians. His irenic attitude left him open to the charge of "wobbling" on the part of the Anglicans and "waffling" by Presbyterians.

Leighton requested that all his papers be destroyed upon his death. In the providence of God, this did not occur. As a result, we may benefit from his treasured exposition of I Peter, printed in 1693 and 1694. His University Lectures *and* Remains *(comprising twenty-seven of his sermons) were reprinted in 1870 and 1875, respectively.*

A Practical Commentary on I Peter

The grace of God in the heart of man is a tender plant in a strange unkindly soil; and therefore cannot well prosper and grow, without much care and pains, and that of a skilful hand . . . For this end, has God given the constant ministry of the word to his Church, not only for the first work of conversion, but also for confirming and increasing of his grace in the hearts of his children.

19

This excellent epistle, full of evangelical doctrine and apostolical authority, is . . . a very clear summary, both of the consolations and instructions needful for the encouragement and direction of a Christian in his journey to heaven.[1]

This is the wisdom of a Christian, when he can solace himself against the meanness of his outward condition, and any kind of discomfort attending it, with the comfortable assurance of the love of God . . . What will it avail a man to be compassed about with the favour of the world, to sit unmolested in his own home and possessions . . . to be well monied, and landed, and befriended, and yet estranged and severed from God, not having any token of his special love?[2]

Did we see how needful Christ is to us, we would esteem and love him more.[3]

The Spirit of God draws a man out of the world by a sanctified light sent into his mind, discovering to him how base and false the sweetness of sin is . . . setting before his eyes the face and happy condition, the glorious liberty of the sons of God . . . making the beauty of Jesus Christ visible to the soul.

Endeavour to have this sanctifying Spirit in yourselves . . . His promise is that he will give the Holy Spirit to them that ask.

Think it not enough that you hear the word, and use the outward ordinances of God, and profess his name; for many are thus called, but a few of them are chosen . . . Make your calling and election sure.[4]

God sees all things from the beginning of time to the end of it, and beyond to all eternity. His foreknowledge is no other than that eternal love of God or decree of election . . . He predestinated, not because he foresaw man would be conformed to Christ, but that they might be so (Rom. 8:29) . . . This foreknowledge, then, is his eternal and unchangeable love.

Effectual calling is inseparably tied to this eternal foreknowledge or election on the one side, and salvation on the other. These two links of the chain are up in heaven, in God's own hand; but this middle one is let down on earth, into the hearts of his children, and they laying hold of it, have sure hold of the other two.[5]

He that loves may be sure he was loved first, and that chooses God for his delight and portion, may conclude confidently that God has chosen him to be one of those who shall enjoy him and be happy in him for ever.

If any claim they have the Spirit, and then turn away from the straight rule of the holy Scripture, they have a spirit indeed, but it is a fanatical spirit, the spirit of delusion and giddiness. But the Spirit of God . . . leads his children in the way of truth [and] squares their thoughts and ways that rule whereof he is the author . . . That inspired word sanctifies them to obedience.[6]

They that are not made saints in the estate of grace shall never be saints in glory.

The title that the saints have to their rich inheritance is of the most valid and unquestionable kind: by birth. By our first natural birth, we are all born to an inheritance indeed—children of wrath, heirs apparent of eternal flames . . . But it is by a new and supernatural birth that men are both freed from their engagement to that woeful inheritance, and invested into the rights of this other . . . as full of happiness as the former is miserable.[7]

It is no doubt a great contentment to the children of God to hear of the excellencies of the life to come . . . Yet there is one doubt [to] be removed . . . The richer the estate is, it will the more kindle the malice and diligence of their enemies, to deprive them of it . . . Against such fears, the apostle comforts the heirs of salvation, assuring them that the estate they look for is certain and safe . . . out of the reach of adverse powers, "reserved in heaven" (I Pet. 1:5) . . . The assurance is full. It is kept for us in heaven, and we [are] kept on earth for it. As it is reserved for us, we are no less surely preserved to it.[8]

The supreme power of God is that on which our stability and perseverance depend . . . Omnipotency supports us, and the everlasting arms are under us. Faith is the second cause of our preservation, because it applies "the power of God." Our faith lays hold upon his power, puts us within those walls, sets the soul within the guard of the power of God, which by self-confidence and vain presuming in its own strength is exposed to all kinds of danger. Faith is a humble, self-denying grace, makes the Christian nothing in himself, and all in God . . . Faith is the victory, and Christ sets his strength against Satan's [as] the great conqueror of the powers of darkness.[9]

When we shall receive that rich and pure and abiding inheritance, that salvation that shall be revealed in the last time, and when time itself shall cease to be, then there shall be no more reckoning of our joys by days and hours, but they shall run parallel with eternity. When all our love, that is scattered and parcelled out upon vanities shall be united and gathered into one and fixed on God, the soul shall be filled with the delight of his presence.

Afflictions . . . are but a transient touch of pain, but that whereon this joy is built is most permanent. The measure of it cannot exceed beyond all hyperbole.[10]

Christ is faithful and true. He has promised to come again, and to judge the world in righteousness . . . He shall judge righteously in that day, who was himself judged unrighteously here on earth. It is called the "revelation." All other things shall be revealed in that day, the most hidden things, good and evil unveiled, but it is eminently the day of his revelation . . . All eyes shall behold him. He shall then gloriously appear before all men and angels, and shall be acknowledged to be the Son of God and judge of the world . . . How beautiful shall he be to those that love him, when he—as the glorious Head—shall appear with his whole body mystical together with him![11]

It is a most unseemly and unpleasant thing to see a man's life full of ups and downs, one step like a Christian, and another like a worldling . . . The very outward vocation of those that profess Christ presses holiness upon them, but the inward far more.

You were running to destruction in the way of sin, and there was a voice together with the gospel preached to your ear, that spake into your heart, and called you back from that path of death to the way of holiness . . . the only way of life . . . It is sacrilege for you to dispose yourselves after the impure manner of the world and apply yourselves to any profane use, whom God has consecrated to himself.[12]

The chief worker of sanctification is the Holy Spirit of God . . . The truth is pure and purifying, yet it cannot of itself purify the soul, but by the obeying or believing it, and the soul cannot obey or believe but by the Spirit . . . This Spirit refines and purifies the soul . . . and sublimates it to the love of God and of his saints, because they are his, and are purified by the same Spirit.

The true reason why there is so little . . . of this Christian mutual love among those that are called Christians is because there is so little of this purifying obedience to the truth . . . Faith unfeigned would beget this love unfeigned. Men may exhort to them both, but they require the hand of God to work them in the heart.[13]

Two things . . . are the very sum of a Christian's duty: to walk as obedient children towards God, and as loving brothers towards one another.

They are children of God by regeneration, and so brothers . . . A new being, a spiritual life, is communicated to them. They have in them their Father's Spirit (Gal. 4:6). They are not only accounted of the family of God by adoption, but by this new birth they are indeed his children.

The gospel [is] the seed of this new birth, because it contains and declares that other Word—the Son of God—as our life . . . That life which shall never end must begin here. It is the new spiritual life whereof the word of God is the immortal seed . . . enduring forever.[14]

Malice and envy are but two branches growing out of the same bitter root. Self-love and evil-speakings are the fruit they bear. Malice is properly the procuring or wishing another's evil; envy, the repining at his good. And these vent themselves by evil-speaking.

This infernal fire within smokes and flashes out by tongue (James 3:6) . . . censuring the actions of those they hate or envy, aggravating their failings and detracting from their virtues.

The art of taking things by the better side, which charity always does, would save much of those janglings and heart-burnings that so abound in the world.[15]

There is this double task in religion . . . A man is not only to be taught true wisdom, but he is to be untaught the errors and wickedness that are deep-rooted in his mind . . . The first work is to raze out these, to cleanse and purify the heart from these blots, these foul characters, that it may receive the impression of the image of God. And because it is the word of God that both begins and advances this work, and perfects the lineaments of that divine image on the soul, therefore receiving this word aright and conforming the soul to Jesus Christ are pre-required for the true growth of the spiritual life.

Hypocrisy and guile stand in opposition to this word that is called the "word of truth."[16]

The life of grace is the proper life of a reasonable soul, and without it the soul is dead . . . The word of God, before called "the immortal seed" is the "milk" of those that are born again. It is very agreeable nourishment to spiritual life.

As a Christian begins to live by the power of the word, he is by nature of that spiritual life directed to that same word as its nourishment . . . Before conversion, wit or eloquence may draw a man to the word, and possibly prove a happy bait to catch him . . . as St. Augustine reports of his hearing St. Ambrose. But when once he is born again, then it is the milk itself he desires, for itself.[17]

To be built on Christ is plainly to believe in him. But in this the most deceive themselves. They hear of great privileges and happiness in Christ, and presently imagine it all theirs, without any more ado . . . We consider not what this is to believe in him, and what is the necessity of this believing, so that we may be partakers of the salvation he has wrought. It is not they that have heard of him, or that have some common knowledge of him, or are able to discourse of him, and speak of his person and nature aright, but "they that believe in him" (I Pet. 2:6) . . . There is in lively faith

. . . a clearer knowledge of Christ and his excellency than before, and with it a recumbency of the soul upon him as the foundation of life and comfort.[18]

You are not ignorant [of] what kind of people they are that have such a knowledge of God as he himself gives; they are enlightened and sanctified by the Spirit, a holy people . . . such as have the riches of his grace, by which they are saved . . . and their heart inflamed with his love . . . They have indeed "obtained mercy" (I Pet. 2:10).

But if you be such as can wallow in the same puddle with the profane world, and take a share of their ungodly ways . . . have your hearts ardent in the love and pursuit of the world, but frozen to God . . . if you can please and delight yourself in any way displeasing to God . . . I can give you no assurance that as yet you have obtained mercy: on the contrary, it is certain that the wrath of God is still abiding on you.[19]

The high mysteries of religion are accompanied with the practical truths which are drawn out of them, as pure streams from a pure stream . . . Upon this model ought the ministers of the gospel to form their preaching . . . To exhort men to holiness and the duties of a Christian life, without instructing them in the doctrine of faith and bringing them to Christ, is to build a house without a foundation. On the other hand, to instruct the mind in the knowledge of divine things and neglect the pressing of the practice and power of godliness, which is the undivided companion of true faith, is to forget the building that ought to be raised upon that foundation once laid, which is likewise a point of very great folly.[20]

A Christian lifestyle has such a beauty that strangers to it . . . cannot choose but love it; and where it begets not love, yet it silences calumny, or at least evinces its falsehood.

The goodness or beauty of a Christian's lifestyle consisting in symmetry and conformity to the word of God as its rule, he ought diligently to study that rule, and to square his ways by it—not to walk at random, but to apply that rule to every step at home and abroad, and to be as careful to keep the beauty of his ways unspotted as those women are of their faces and attire, that are most studious of comeliness.

This is the purest and highest kind of godly fear, that springs from love.[21]

This fear of God . . . has chiefly three things: a reverent esteem of the Majesty of God, which is a fundamental thing in religion, that moulds the heart most powerfully to the obedience of his will; a firm belief in the purity of God, and of his power and justice; a right apprehension of the bitterness of his wrath, and the sweetness of his love; sovereign love to God, for his own infinite excellency and goodness; a most earnest desire to please him in all things . . . a holy fear lest we should sin, and a watchfulness that we sin not, and deep sorrow and speedy returning and humbling before him when we have sinned.[22]

The behaviour [of this suffering Christ] was intended for an example. He left his footsteps as a copy, to be followed by us. Every step of his is a letter of this copy . . . a pure and perfect copy of obedience in clear and great letters, in his own blood. His whole life is our rule: his obedience, holiness, meekness, and humility, are our copy.

If we neglect his example set before us, we cannot enjoy any right assurance of his sufferings for us . . . The apostle refers to the words of that Evangelist among the Prophets, Isaiah 53:4, about his bearing "our sins in his own body on the tree . . ." This was his business—not only to rectify sinful man by his example, but to redeem him by his blood.[23]

A Christian husband and wife are equally co-heirs of the same "grace of life" (I Pet. 3:7). This is that which most strongly binds on all these duties, on the hearts of husbands and wives, and most strongly indeed binds their hearts together and makes them one . . . Hearts focused on him are most excellently one. That love which is cemented by youth and beauty, when these moulder and decay, it fades too . . . The ignorance or disregard of this is the true cause of so much bitterness or so little true sweetness in the life of most married persons, because God is left out and they meet not as one in him.[24]

A purified heart will unteach the tongue all filthy impure speeches, and will give it a holy strain; and the spirit of charity and humility will banish that mischievous disposition that sits so deep in most, of reproaching and disgracing others . . . It is wicked self-love and pride of heart whence those do spring . . . [Beware of] that flux of the tongue, that prating and babbling disease.

Divert the tongue from evil, and guide by a habit of, and delight in, profitable and gracious discourse . . . such speech as "may edify and administer grace to the hearers" (Eph. 4:29) . . . In this humble, sincere way, you too shall grow in grace and in knowledge.[25]

When you address yourself to prayer, desire and depend upon the inspiration of the Holy Spirit of God—without which you are not able truly to pray. It is a supernatural work, and therefore the principle of it must be supernatural. He that has nothing of the Spirit of God cannot pray at all. He may howl as a beast in his necessity or distress. Or he may speak words of prayer, as some birds learn the language of men, but pray he cannot.

Learn to keep a watchful eye over your own hearts throughout every step of the way . . . by keeping up a continual remembrance of the presence of God . . . from beginning to end, keep sight of him.[26]

Seek to have the Lord in your hearts and sanctify him there. He shall make them strong, and carry them through all dangers (Ps. 23:4) . . . What is it that makes the Church so firm and stout? It is this: "God is in the midst of her" (Ps. 46:2–5). He is immovable, and establishes all where he resides. If the world be in the middle of the heart, it will be often shaken, for there is continual motion and change, but God in it keeps it stable. Labour, therefore, to get God into your hearts, residing in the midst of them, in the midst of all conditions, they shall not move.[27]

Faith is the root of all graces, and of all obedience and holiness . . . Hope looks out for [the fulfilment] of divine promises. The gospel, being held by faith, provides a hope that has substance and reality in it.

The work of grace may evidence to you the truth of your hope; but the ground it fastens on is Jesus Christ, in whom all our rights and evidences hold good: his death assuring us of freedom from condemnation, and his life and possession of glory being the foundation of our hope (Heb. 6:19). If you would have it immutable, rest it there. Lay all this hope on him, and when assaulted fetch all your answers for it from him. For it is "Christ in you" that is your "hope of glory" (Col. 1:27).[28]

That we may wholly live to "the will of God," we must first know what his will is. Persons grossly ignorant of God, and of his will, cannot live to him . . . That knowledge is . . . the first part of the renewed image of God . . . a beam of God's own, issuing from himself, both enlightening and enlivening the whole soul. It gains the affection and stirs to action . . . The more we walk according to what we know of the will of God, the more we shall be advanced to know more . . . As Divine knowledge begets this affection, so this affection will bring forth action, real obedience . . . Thus renewed, the living Christian is all for God, a sacrifice entirely offered up to God, "a living sacrifice."[29]

The graces of the Spirit are an entire frame, making up the new creature, and none of them can be missing; therefore the doctrine and exhortation of the Apostles speak of them usually not only as inseparable, but as one. But among them all, none is more comprehensive than love . . . "the fulfilling of the law" (Rom. 13:10). Love to God is the sum of all relative to him, and so likewise is it towards our brethren. Love . . . most powerfully weans us from this world and causes us to delight in communion with him, in holy meditation and prayer.[30]

The devil, being an apostate spirit, revolted and separated from God, does naturally project and work division. This was his first exploit, and is still his grand design and business in the world. He first divided men from God; put them at enmity by the first sin of our first parents; and the next we read of regarding their first child was enmity against his brother. So Satan is called by our Saviour, justly, a "liar" and a "murderer" from the beginning (John 8:44). He murdered man by lying, and made him a murderer.[31]

As the devil's work is division, Christ's work is union. He came to dissolve the works of the devil (I John 3:8), by a contrary work. He came to make all friends; to recollect and reunite all men to God, and man to man . . . This was his great project in all. For this he died and suffered. For this he prayed (John 17). Union in Christ is strong above all ties, natural or civil. If natural friendship be capable of that expression, "one spirit in two bodies," Christian union demonstrates it more truly and properly—there is indeed one Spirit, more extensive in all the faithful . . . They are not so much diverse bodies, but only diverse members of one body.[32]

When we consider this fighting life aright, we need not be dissuaded from loving it. We rather have need to be strengthened with patience to go through and to fight on with courage and assurance of victory; still fighting in a higher strength than our own, against sin within and troubles without. This is the great scope of this epistle. Against *sin*, the Apostle instructs us at the beginning of this chapter. And here again against *suffering* . . . He urges us to be armed with the same mind that was in Christ . . . The words to the end of the chapter contain grounds of encouragement and consolation for the children of God in sufferings, especially in suffering for God.[33]

It is an excellent life, and the proper life of a Christian, to be daily outstripping himself, to be spiritually wiser, holier, more heavenly-minded . . . Every day loving the world less, and Christ more.

The well-instructed "looks to Jesus" (Heb. 12:2), looks away from all oppositions and difficulties, looks above them to Jesus— the Author and Finisher of our faith . . . Thus that royal dignity is interested in the maintenance and completion of what he has wrought. Notwithstanding all your imperfections, and the strength of sin, he can and will subdue it . . . Though you are weak, he is strong . . . and renews your strength (Isa. 40:28–31).[34]

THREE

✣ RICHARD SIBBES ✣

1 5 7 7 — 1 6 3 5

---

*"The analysis of the conversion process first became a prominent topic of
Puritan thought in the work of such men as Richard Rodgers, Arthur
Hildersam, William Perkins, and Richard Sibbes."*[1]

*Sibbes was educated at Cambridge, and preached at Gray's Inn. It
was said that heaven was in him before he was in heaven. Yet he was ha-
rassed by the political and ecclesiastical authorities, severely reprimanded,
pressured to conform, and denounced as a dangerous conspirator.
Whether expounding doctrine or exhorting hearers to do their duty, he ad-
dressed himself with warm pastoral sensitivity to the mind, will, and affections of his people.*

Richard Baxter owed his spiritual awakening to The Bruised Reed
and Smoking Flax, *produced by Sibbes in 1630. Also from this
preacher's gifted pen are* The Soul's Conflict *(1635),* The Returning
Backslider *(1639),* A Description of Christ *(1639), and* A Learned
Commentary on II Corinthians, Chapter 1 *(1655).*

A Description of Christ

It is usual in the prophecies, especially of Isaiah, that evangelical
prophet, when he foretells anything comfortable to the people in
the promise of temporal things, he rises to confirm their faith in
better things by adding thereto a prophecy and a promise of Christ
the Messiah.

Christ is called a servant . . . in respect of his condition (Phil. 2:7). Christ took upon him the form of a servant; he emptied himself; he was the lowest of all servants in condition: none was ever as abased as our glorious Saviour.

Christ . . . was an ambassador sent from the great God: a prophet, a priest, and a king . . . to bring God and man together again.[2]

There was first in Christ human flesh, abased flesh, and then glorious flesh. Abasement was first necessary for Christ; he could not have performed the office of a servant, unless he had undertaken the condition of a servant. He must first be abased and then glorious, our ill must be his before his good could be ours. And how could he undergo our ill, our sin and misery, and the curse due to us, unless abased? Our sins must be imputed to him, and then his righteousness and whatsoever is good is ours; so here is both the abasement of his condition and the excellency of his office to be a king, priest and prophet to his Church.[3]

Christ stood not upon his greatness, but, being equal with God, he became a servant. Oh! we should dismount from the tower of our conceited excellency. . . . We should descend from the heaven of our conceit, and take upon us the form of servants, and abase ourselves to do good to others . . . A Christian is the greatest freeman in the world; he is free from the wrath of God, free from hell and damnation, from the curse of the law. But then, though he be free in these respects, yet in regard of love he is the greatest servant. Love abases him to do all the good he can. And the more the Spirit of Christ is in us, the more it will abase us to anything wherein we can be serviceable.[4]

God in paradise did choose a wife for Adam, so God has chosen a husband for his church. He has chosen Christ for us. Therefore, it is intolerable sacrilegious rebellion and impudence to refuse a Saviour and Mediator of God's choosing, and set up others of our own—as if we were wiser to choose for ourselves than God is . . . Let God's choice and ours agree.[5]

This is our comfort and our confidence, that God accepts us because he accepts his beloved. And when he shall cease to love Christ, he shall cease to love the members of Christ . . . God loves us with that inseparable love wherewith he loves his own Son (Rom. 8:35ff.).[6]

You see what a wondrous confidence and comfort we have hence, if we labour to be in Christ, that then God loves and delights in us, because he loves and delights in Christ Jesus.[7]

In our daily approach to God . . . we go to God in the name of the one he loves, "in whom his soul delights."[8]

God loves and delights in him for the work of salvation and redemption by his blood. Shall we not love and embrace him for his love which is for our good?[9]

We should therefore desire God to shed the love of Christ into our hearts more and more, that we may feel in our souls the love that he bears to us.[10]

A man may know that he is in Christ, if he find the Spirit of Christ in him . . . There is one Spirit in the head and in the members . . . Now this Spirit is renewing (II Cor. 5:17) . . . If there be no change in us, we have no present interest in Christ.

The very beholding of Christ is a transforming sight. The Spirit who makes us new creatures and stirs us up to behold this servant, is a transforming beholding. If we look upon him with the eye of faith, it will make us like Christ. For the gospel is a mirror . . . When we look into it, we are changed from glory to glory (II Cor. 3:18) . . . When we see the love of God in the gospel, and the love of Christ giving himself for us, this will transform us to love God.[11]

There are three main defects in man since the fall: ignorance and blindness; rebellion in will and affections; and a subjection to the wrath of God and eternal damnation . . . Whosoever shall be ordained a Saviour must provide appropriate remedies for these. Hereupon comes a threefold office in Christ . . . to cure this threefold mischief and malady.

As we are ignorant and blind, he is a *prophet* to instruct us, to convince us of the ill state we are in, and then to convince us of the good he intends for us, and has wrought for us, to instruct us in all things concerning our everlasting comfort . . . He opens the heart, he teaches us to do the things he teaches . . . to love and to obey.[12]

Answerable to the rebellion and sinfulness of our dispositions, he is a *king* to subdue whatever is ill in us, and likewise to subdue all opposite power outside us. By little and little, he will trample all enemies under his feet, and under our feet, too, ere long.

Now, as we are cursed by reason of our sinful condition, so he is *priest* to satisfy the wrath of God for us (Gal. 3:13). He became a servant, that he might die and undergo the death of the cross; not only death, but a cursed death, and so his blood might be an atonement as a priest.

So, answerable to the threefold ill in us, you see here is a threefold office in Christ.[13]

Now the fundamental, the chief office to which he was anointed by the Spirit—upon which the rest depends—was his priestly office. Wherefore was his teaching, but to instruct us what he must do and suffer for us, and what benefit we have by his sacrifice: reconciliation with God, and freedom from the wrath of God, and right to life everlasting, by his obedience to the cursed death of the cross? And how does he come to be a king to rule over us by his Holy Spirit, and to have a claim on us, but because as priest he first died for us?

Whatever we have from God is especially from the great work of Christ as a priest abasing himself, and dying for us.[14]

A priest was to offer sacrifice and to pray for his people. Our Saviour did both in the days of his humiliation, in his prayer in John 17. There, as a priest, he commends his sacrifice to God before he died; and now he is in heaven making intercession for us, to the end of the world. He appears for us there.

We see, then, to what purpose God put the Spirit upon Christ, to enable him to be a prophet, a priest, and a king, and thus take away those mischiefs and evils to which we were subject and enslaved; so that we have a supply for all that may in any way abase us and cast us down, in the all-sufficiency that is in Christ Jesus, who was anointed with the Spirit for this end.[15]

How does Christ give his Spirit to us? This Spirit, so necessary for us, is given by the ministry of the gospel, which is the ministry of the Spirit (Gal. 3:2). When the love of God in Christ and the benefits by Christ are laid open in the preaching of the gospel to us, God gives his Holy Spirit, the Spirit of Christ. Now God in Christ would save us by a triumphant and abundant love and mercy, and the Spirit of God never goes but where there is a magnifying of the love and mercy of God in Christ. Therefore, the ministry of the gospel, which alone discovers the amity and love of God to mankind, being now reconciled in Christ, is accompanied with the Spirit . . . Christ is the first gift, and the Spirit is the second.[16]

If we would have the Spirit of God, let us attend upon the sweet promises of salvation, upon the doctrine of Christ, because together with the knowledge of these things, the Holy Ghost slides and insinuates and infuses himself into our souls. Therefore, the ministers of the gospel should be much in laying open the riches of God in Christ. In unfolding Christ, all other things will follow.

Those ages wherein the Spirit of God is most, is where Christ is most preached. People are best always where there is most Spirit; and they are most joyful and comfortable and holy, where Christ is truly laid open to the hearts of the people.[17]

The Holy Spirit is given to them that obey, to them that do not resist the Spirit of God . . . If we would have the Spirit of Christ, let us labour to subject ourselves to the Spirit . . . Give way to the motions of God's Spirit . . . Turn not back those blessed messengers, let us entertain them, let the Spirit dwell and rule in us. The Spirit is the most blessed lodger that we ever entertained in all our lives. If we let the Spirit guide and rule us, he will lead us and govern and support us in life and death, and never leave us till he shall have raised our bodies (Rom. 8:11) . . . and brought us to heaven.

Another means whereby we come to obtain the Spirit is prayer (Luke 11:13) . . . God can give nothing greater nor can we beg nothing greater, if we have sanctified judgments.[18]

All grace comes by declaring. "The gospel is the power of God to salvation" (Rom. 1:16) Let the gospel—which is God's judgment as to how men shall be saved, and how they shall walk in obedience by way of thankfulness to God—be declared. Then all that belong to God shall come in, and yield homage to it, and be brought in subjection. The devil . . . knows this well enough. Therefore, he labours to hinder the declaration of judgment [the word of God] by all means. He will not have God's judgments but men's traditions declared. He knows the declaring of God's judgments will quickly breed a change in men's dispositions . . . They shall yield spiritual obedience and come in and be saved.[19]

The Bruised Reed

The prophet Isaiah being lifted up and carried with the wing of prophetical spirit, passes over all the time between him and the appearing of Jesus Christ in the flesh, and sees with the eye of prophecy, and the eye of faith, Christ as present (Isa. 42:1–4; Matt. 12:18–21) . . . to deal with bruised reeds and smoking flax.[20]

The bruised reed is a man that for the most part is in some misery, as those were that came to Christ for help, and by misery is brought to see sin as the cause of it . . . he is sensible of sin and misery, even unto bruising; and seeing no help in himself, is carried with restless desire to have supply from another, with some hope . . . of mercy. This spark of hope being opposed by doubtings, and fears rising from corruption, makes him as smoking flax.[21]

This bruising is required *before* conversion, so that the Spirit may make way for himself with the heart by levelling all proud, high thoughts and that we may understand ourselves to be what indeed we are by nature . . . This bruising makes us set a high price on Christ. The gospel is then the gospel indeed . . . It makes us more thankful, and more fruitful in our lives . . . What makes many so cold and barren, but that bruising for sin never endeared God's grace to them? Nay, *after* conversion we need bruising, that reeds may know themselves to be reeds and not oaks.[22]

Christ will not break the bruised reed. Consider his very name, Jesus, Saviour, who comes to heal the broken-hearted (Isa. 61:1) and "all that are weary and heavy laden" (Matt. 11:28).[23]

Are you bruised? Be of good comfort. He calls you. Conceal not your wounds, open all before him, keep not Satan's counsel. Go to Christ though trembling, as the poor woman, if we can but "touch the hem of his garment," (Matt. 9:20) we shall be healed and have a gracious answer. Go boldly to God in our flesh; for this end that we might go boldly to him, he is flesh of our flesh, and bone of our bone. Never fear to go to God, since we have such a Mediator with him, who is not only our friend, but our brother and husband . . . Let the world be as it will, if we cannot rejoice in the world, yet we may "rejoice in the Lord" (Phil. 4:4).[24]

God will not quench the smoking flax, but blow it up till it flames. In smoking flax there is but little light . . . Grace is little at the first . . . Let us not be discouraged at the small beginnings of grace, but look on ourselves as "elected to be blameless and without spot" (Eph. 1:4) . . . Christ will not quench small and weak beginnings. First, because this spark is from heaven, it is his own, it is kindled by his own spirit. And secondly, it tends to the glory of his powerful grace in his children that he preserves light in the midst of darkness—a spark in the midst of the swelling waters of corruption.[25]

Men must not be too curious in prying into the weaknesses of others. We should labour rather to see what they have that is for eternity, to incline our hearts to love them, than into that weakness which the Spirit of God will in time consume, to estrange us. Some think it strength of grace to endure nothing in the weaker, whereas the strongest are readiest to bear with the infirmities of the weak.

The Holy Ghost is content to dwell in smoky, offensive souls. Oh that the Spirit would breathe into our spirits the like merciful disposition!

The Church is a common hospital, wherein all are in some measure sick of some spiritual disease . . . We should all have ground of exercising mutually the spirit of wisdom and meekness.[26]

We must have two eyes, one to see imperfections in ourselves and others; the other to see what is good . . . They will ever lack comfort that are much in quarrelling with themselves, and through their infirmities are prone to feed upon such bitter things as will most nourish the very distemper they are sick of. These delight to be looking only on the dark side of the cloud.[27]

So far as a man is spiritual, so far is light delightful to him, as willing to see anything amiss, that he may reform, and any further service discovered that he may perform, because he truly hates evil and loves good.[28]

Since Christ is thus comfortably set out to us, let us not believe Satan's [mis]representations of him. When we are troubled in conscience for our sins, his manner is then to present him to the afflicted soul as a most severe judge armed with justice against us. But then let us present him to our souls as offered to our view by God himself, as holding out a sceptre of mercy, and spreading his arms to receive us . . . In Christ all perfections of mercy and love meet. How great must that mercy be that lodges in so gracious a heart?

We are weak, but we are his; we are deformed, but yet bear his image . . . Christ finds matter of love from that which is his own in us.[29]

Considering this gracious nature in Christ, let us think with ourselves thus: When he is so kind to us, shall we be cruel against him in his name, in his truth, in his children?

This mercy of Christ should move us to commiserate the state of the poor church, torn by enemies without, and rending itself by divisions at home . . . Unless you will disclaim all consolation in Christ (Phil. 2:1–4), labour to maintain the unity of the Spirit in the bond of peace. What a joyful spectacle is this to Satan and his faction, to see those that are separated from the world fall in pieces among themselves! Our discord is the enemy's melody.[30]

The same Spirit that convinces us of the necessity of his righteousness to cover us, convinces us also of the necessity of his government to rule us. His love to us moves him to dispose us to be like himself, and our love to him stirs us up to be such as he may take delight in.

It is one main fruit of Christ's exaltation that he may turn every one of us from our wickedness (Acts 3:26).

Discern who may lay just claim to Christ's mercy: only those who will take his yoke, and count it a greater happiness to be under his government than to enjoy any liberty of the flesh.[31]

Christ's Spirit must subdue our hearts, and sanctify them to love him, without which all motive would be ineffectual. Our disposition must be changed, we must be new creatures; they seek for heaven in hell that seek for spiritual love in an unchanged heart . . . It is natural for a child of God to love Christ so far as he is renewed, from an inward principle and work of grace . . . First, we are made partakers of the divine nature, and then we are easily induced and led by Christ's Spirit to spiritual duties.

The spiritual government of Christ in us is joined with judgment and wisdom. Wherever true spiritual wisdom and judgment are, there likewise the Spirit of Christ brings in his gracious government.[32]

Truth is truth, and error, error. That which is unlawful is unlawful, whether men think so or not. God has put an eternal difference between light and darkness, good and evil, which no creature's conceit can alter; and therefore no man's judgment is the measure of things further than it agrees to the truth stamped upon things themselves by God.[33]

Where grace has brought the heart under, there unruly passions do not cast such a mist before the understanding, but that in particular it sees that which is best.

Men of an ill governed life have no true judgment: no wicked man can be a wise man.[34]

Christ has conquered all in his own person, first, and he is God over all, blessed for evermore; and therefore over sin, death, hell, Satan and the world. And as he has overcome them in himself, so he overcomes them in our hearts and consciences.

Christ sets up his kingdom in the conscience, and makes it a kind of paradise.

The Spirit of truth, to whose tuition Christ has committed his Church, and the truth of the Spirit which is the sceptre of Christ, abide forever . . . This truth must not only live forever, but likewise prevail over all that oppose it, for both the word and the Spirit are mighty in operation (Heb. 4:12) . . . A little faith strengthened by Christ will work wonders.[35]

Christ as king brings in a commanding light into the soul . . . The end of Christ's coming was to destroy the works of the devil, both for us and in us. And the end of the resurrection was: to quicken our souls from death in sin; to free our souls from such snares and sorrows of spiritual death as accompany the guilt of sin; to raise them up . . . as the sun breaks forth more gloriously out of a thick cloud; to raise us out of particular slips and failings, stronger; to raise us out of all troublesome and dark conditions of this life; and at length to raise our bodies out of the dust.[36]

The same power that the Spirit showed in raising Christ our head from the sorrows of death . . . will the Spirit show in the church, which is his body.[37]

When chaff strives against the wind, stubble against the fire, when the heel kicks against the goads, when the clay strives with the potter, when man strives against God, it is easy to know on which side the victory will go. The winds may toss the ship wherein Christ is, but not overturn it. The waves may dash against the rock, but they do but break themselves against it.[38]

Yet the victory seems to go with the enemy. Why? God's children usually in their troubles overcome by suffering . . . This victory is by degrees . . . Christ's work, both in the church and in the hearts of Christians, often goes backward that it may go the better forward . . . Weakness with watchfulness will stand out, when strength with too much confidence fails.[39]

Some have, after conflict, wondered at the goodness of God, that so little and shaking faith should have upheld them in so great combats, when Satan had almost caught them. And, indeed, it is to be wondered how much a little grace will prevail with God for acceptance, and over our enemies for victory, if the heart be right. Such is the goodness of our sweet Saviour, that he delights still to show his strength in our weakness.[40]

Grace conquers us first, and we by it conquer all things—whether it be corruptions within us, or temptations without us.

"Everyone that is born of God overcomes the world" (I John 5:4).[41]

The way to prevail is to get the victory over the pride of our own nature, by taking shame to ourselves, in humble confession to God; to overcome the unbelief of our hearts, by yielding to the promise of pardon; to set ourselves against those sins which have prevailed over us, in confidence of Christ's assistance. Then, prevailing over ourselves, we shall easily prevail over all our enemies.[42]

There will be more glorious times when "the kingdoms of the earth shall be the Lord Jesus Christ's" (Rev. 11:15), and he shall reign for ever; then shall judgment and truth have their victory; then Christ will plead his own cause.[43]

The spirit of antichrist is now lifted up, and marches furiously. But our comfort is that Christ lives and reigns and stands on Mount Zion in defense of them that stand for him.[44]

FOUR

❧ THOMAS WATSON ❧

DIED 1689

This eminent nonconformist divine prepared for ministry at Emmanuel College, Cambridge. He became rector of St. Stephen's, Wallbrook, London, in 1646. Thomas Watson experienced ejection in 1662, but continued preaching at Crosby Hall and elsewhere. An impressive preacher of the Word, Watson held strong Presbyterian convictions and yet retained high regard for the king during those tumultuous times of civil war.

Watson's published works include The Saint's Delight *(1657),* The Art of Divine Contentment *(1653), A* Discourse on Meditation *(1660), and* One Hundred and Seventy Six Sermons on the Lesser Catechism *(also known as* Practical Divinity*), printed posthumously in 1692.*

Practical Divinity

The ten commandments are the rule of our life, the creed is the sum of our faith, and the Lord's prayer is the pattern of our prayer . . . So let all your petitions agree and symbolize with the things contained in the Lord's prayer . . . Tertullian calls it a breviary and compendium of the gospel . . . Never was there prayer so admirably composed as this.[1]

The prayer [begins with] a preface: "Our Father which art in heaven" . . . We must address ourselves in prayer to God alone: The Father, the Son, and the Holy Ghost . . .

God, that he might encourage us to pray to him, represents himself under this sweet notion of a Father. The name Jehovah carries majesty in it, the name of Father carries mercy in it.

God is a Father by creation . . . we are his offspring (Acts 17:28; Mal. 2:10) . . . God is a Father by election (Eph. 1:4), by special grace . . . He consecrates the elect by his Spirit and infuses in them a supernatural principle of holiness, therefore they are said to be born of God (I John 3:9). Only such as are sanctified can say, "Our Father which art in heaven."[2]

We are "children of God by faith in Christ Jesus" (Gal. 3:26). . . . God is the Father of Christ; faith makes us Christ's brothers, and so God comes to be our Father (Heb. 2:11).[3]

God is the best Father . . . because he is perfect, wise, and most loving (I John 4:16).[4]

We honour our Father in heaven by having a reverential awe (Lev. 25:17) . . . and by resembling him (Col. 3:10) in holiness . . . If God be our Father, then we love to be near God and have converse with him . . . He who has God for his Father, has God for his pattern.[5]

To pray in faith is to pray for that which God has promised. Where there is no promise, we cannot pray in faith . . . To pray in Christ's name is to pray in the hope of confidence in Christ's merit.[6]

In this petition, "Hallowed be thy name," we pray that God's name may shine forth gloriously and that it may be honoured and sanctified by us, in the whole course and tenor of our lives.[7]

By God's name is meant anything by which God may be known . . . We hallow and sanctify God's name when we profess his name . . . have a high appreciation and esteem of God . . . trust in his name . . . love his name . . . and give him a holy and spiritual worship . . . by obeying him. How does a son more honour his father, than by obedience? (Ps. 40:8).[8]

A soul truly devoted to God joins heartily in this petition, "Thy kingdom come" (Matt. 6:10) . . . God is a king . . . a great king

... a glorious king ... If God be such an absolute monarch, crowned with such glory and majesty, let us all engage in his service, stand up for his truth and worship.[9]

The kingdom of grace is nothing but the beginning of the kingdom of glory ... The kingdom of grace is glory militant, and the kingdom of glory is grace triumphant ... Let us pray that Satan's kingdom, set up in the world, may be thrown down [and] that the kingdom of grace may be set up in our hearts and increased.[10]

How may we know the kingdom of grace is set up in us? By having a change wrought in the soul (II Cor. 5:17) ... When the kingdom of grace is set up, there is a light in the mind, order in the affections, pliableness of the will, tenderness in the conscience ... we may know the kingdom of grace is come to us, by antipathy and opposition against every known sin (Ps. 119:104).[11]

This glory in the kingdom of heaven shall be begun at death, but not perfected until the resurrection ... Heaven is not only a kingdom which God has promised, but which Christ has purchased (Eph. 1:14) with the price of his blood (Heb. 10:19) ... The elect must have this blessed kingdom by virtue of their coalition and union with Jesus Christ. They are members of Christ, therefore they must be where their head is. Can Christ lose a member of his body?[12]

We must pray earnestly that the kingdom of glory may come, that we may see God "face to face" and have uninterrupted and eternal communion with him in the empyrean heaven.[13]

The third petition, "Thy will be done on earth as it is in heaven" (Matt. 6:10), consists of two parts: the matter, doing God's will; the manner, as it is in heaven.

What is meant by the will of God? God's revealed will, written in the book of Scripture, [which makes known] what he would have us do in order to our salvation. [So] we pray for active obedience, that we may do God's will actively in what he commands, and submit to God's will patiently in what he inflicts ... We must know

God's will before we can do it; knowledge is the eye which must direct the foot of obedience.[14]

'Tis improper to call such Christians, who are knowers of God's will but not doers of it . . . If God give us our allowance, we should give him our allegiance . . . All God's royal edicts and precepts are to bring us to be doers of his will . . . The word of God is not only a rule of knowledge, but of duty (Deut. 13:4) . . . All that is written in the law or the gospel tends to this, that we shall be doers of God's will. By doing the will of God, we evidence sincerity . . . and propagate the gospel . . . and show our love to Christ (John 14:21) . . . Not to do God's will on earth is sinful, foolish and dangerous.[15]

Whatever God wills us to do is for our benefit (Deut. 10:12, 13) . . . It is God's will that we should repent, and this is for our good, [since] repentance ushers in remission . . . It is God's will that we should believe, that we should be crowned with salvation . . . What God wills is not so much our duty, as our privilege.

To do God's will on earth makes us like Christ, and akin to Christ . . . [who] did his Father's will (John 6:38; 4:34) . . . Doing God's will on earth brings peace in life and death . . . Doing God's will, will be both your comfort and your crown.[16]

The manner of doing God's will is the chief thing . . . We must not only do *what* God appoints, but *as* God appoints . . . We do God's will acceptably when we do duties spiritually—from an inward principle—a renewed principle of grace . . . The inward principle of obedience is faith . . . Faith looks at Christ in every duty, it touches the hem of his garment; and through Christ, both the person and the offering are accepted (Eph. 1:6).[17]

We do God's will acceptably when we prefer his will before all other (Acts 4:19); when we do it as it is done by the angels in heaven (Ps. 103:20) . . . willingly, fervently, swiftly, and constantly.[18]

Let us examine all our actions whether they are according to God's will. The will of God is the rule and standard . . . it is the sundial by which we must set all our actions . . . Are your speeches according to God's will? Are our words savory, being seasoned with grace? Are we patterns of prudence and piety? Do we keep up the credit of religion, and shine as lights in the world?[19]

Let us get humble hearts. Pride is the spring of disobedience (Ex. 5:2) . . . The humble soul says, "Lord, what will you have me to do?" He puts, as it were, a blank cheque into God's hand and bids him write what he will, and he will subscribe to it.[20]

Murmuring is incompatible with submission to God's will; murmuring is the height of impatience, it is a kind of mutiny in the soul against God (Num. 21:5) Murmuring is very evil. It springs from pride, and distrust of God's promises.

When the strings of the lute are snarled, the lute can make no good music: so, when a Christian's spirits are perplexed and disturbed, he cannot make melody in his heart to the Lord.[21]

Patient submission to God's will is a gracious frame of soul, whereby a Christian is content to be at God's disposal, and acquiesces in his wisdom.[22]

The fourth petition in the Lord's prayer: "Give us this day our daily bread" (Matt. 6:11). First we pray, "Hallowed by thy name, thy kingdom come, thy will be done." Hence we learn that the glory of God ought to be preferred before our own personal concerns . . . But before there can be a preferring of God's glory before our private concerns, there must be a new birth wrought. The natural man seeks his own secular interests before God's glory . . . A worm cannot fly and sing as a lark: a natural man, whose heart creeps upon the earth, cannot admire God or advance his glory, as does a man elected by grace.[23]

"Give us this day our daily bread." The sum of this petition is that God would give us such a competency in these outward things as he sees most excellent for us (Prov. 30:8) . . . The good things of this life are the gifts of God: he is the donor of all our blessings (James 1:17) . . . Wisdom and riches are his gifts, so are peace and health—which is the cream of life (Jer. 30:17) . . . All we have is from the hand of God's royal bounty; we have nothing but what God gives us out of his store-house; we cannot have but one bit of bread but from God.[24]

The tree of mercy will not drop its fruit, unless shaken by the hand of prayer . . . How wicked are they, who instead of going to God for food when they lack, they go to the devil; they make a compact with him, and if he will help them to a livelihood, they will give them their souls. Better starve, than go to the devil for provender.

Whatever we receive from God is a gift. We can give nothing to God but what he has given to us (I Chron. 29:14) . . . If all be a gift, then merit is exploded, and shut out of doors.[25]

If all be a gift, see then the odious ingratitude of men, who sin against their giver. God feeds them, and they fight against him; he gives them bread, and they give him affronts . . . Ungratefully do sinners deal with God. They not only forget his mercies, but abuse them (Jer. 5:7) . . . This gives a dye and tincture to men's sins, and makes them crimson.

God gives us daily bread, let us give him daily praise. Thankfulness to our donor is the best policy . . . God loves to bestow his mercies where there is the best echo of praise.[26]

In praying for spiritual things, we must be absolute. When we pray for pardon of sin, and the favour of God, and the sanctifying graces of the Spirit, these are indispensably necessary to salvation, and here we must take no denial. But when we pray for temporal things, here our prayers must be limited, we must pray conditionally so far as God sees them good for us. God sometimes sees cause to withhold temporal things from us: they may be snares, and draw our hearts from God, therefore we must pray for these things with submission to God's will.[27]

When we pray for things pertaining to this life, we must desire temporal things for spiritual ends; we must desire these things to be as helps in our journey to heaven. If we pray for health, it must be that we may improve this talent of health for God's glory, and may be fitter for his service . . . If we are to pray for temporal good things, then how much more for spiritual? If we are to pray for bread, then how much more for the bread of life? If we pray to have our hunger satisfied, much more should we pray to have our souls saved . . . Therefore, let us be earnest for spiritual mercies.[28]

The fifth petition in the Lord's prayer is this: "And forgive us our debts, as we forgive our debtors" (Matt. 6:12) . . . Though we have daily bread, yet it will do us no good unless sins be forgiven . . . Daily bread may satisfy our appetite, but forgiveness satisfies the conscience.

Forgiveness is the sauce that would make our bread relish the sweeter.

Daily bread may make us live comfortably, but forgiveness of sin will make us die comfortably . . . Besides daily bread, get pardon of sin.[29]

Sin is debt, and every sinner is a debtor. Why is sin called a debt? Because it fitly resembles it . . . We owe to God exact obedience, and not paying what is due, we come to be in debt . . . By our sins, we become guilty, and stand obliged to God's curse of damnation.

We have nothing [with which] to pay. We can pay neither principal nor interest. Adam made us all bankrupts. In innocency Adam had a stock of original righteousness . . . He could give God personal and perfect obedience. But by his sin, he is quite broken, and has beggared all his posterity.[30]

Sin is the worst debt, because it is against an infinite majesty. It is a multiplied debt. We do not know how much we owe God . . . But God writes down our debts in his book of remembrance. God's book, and the book of conscience do exactly agree, so that this debt cannot be denied.

There is no shifting of the debt . . . Neither man nor angel can pay this debt for us. Who shall give us protection from God's justice? We cannot flee from God . . . He knows where to find all his debtors (Ps. 139:7, 8) . . . There is a day coming when God will call his debtors to account (Rom. 14:12).[31]

Let us confess our debts, and pray for the forgiveness of our sins (Luke 11:4). This forgiveness is God's passing by sin (Mic. 7:18), wiping off the score, and giving us a discharge.

God, in pardoning, lifts our burden from the conscience and lays it upon Christ (Isa. 53:6). To forgive is to cover sin (Ps. 32:1), to blot out transgression (Isa. 43:25) . . . When God forgives sin, he blots out the debt, he draws the red line of Christ's blood over our sins, and so crosses the debt-book. . . . Sin is the cloud interposed, but God dispels the cloud, and breaks forth with the light of his countenance. . . . He casts our sins into the depths of the sea (Mic. 7:19).[32]

Forgiveness of sin is purely an act of God's free grace . . . When God pardons a sin, he does not pay a debt, but gives a legacy . . . Forgiveness is through the blood of Christ—the outward cause meriting pardon (Eph. 1:7) . . . The guilt of sin was infinite, and nothing but that blood which was of infinite value could procure forgiveness . . . God's free grace found a way of redemption through a Mediator.

By virtue of this pardon, God will no more call sin into remembrance (Heb. 8:12) . . . But sin is not forgiven till it be repented of. Therefore repentance and remission are put together (Luke 24:47).[33]

In repentance there are three main ingredients, and all these must be before forgiveness: contrition, confession, conversion.

Faith necessarily precedes forgiveness. There must be believing on our part, before there is forgiving on God's part (Acts 10:43). There are two acts of faith—to accept Christ and his terms, and to trust in his merits . . . Without faith, no remission.[34]

We imitate God in forgiving them that trespass against us— when we strive against all thoughts of revenge, wish well to them, grieve at their calamities, seek reconciliation with them, and show ourselves ready to receive them: this is gospel forgiving.[35]

The sixth petition in the Lord's prayer: "And lead us not into temptation, but deliver us from evil" (Matt. 6:13). Does God lead us into temptation? God tempts no man to sin (James 1:13). God may permit sin, but does not promote it. He who is an encourager of holiness cannot be a patron of sin . . . There is a great deal of difference between God's testing his people's grace and exciting their corruptions.

We desire of God that he would not allow us to be overcome by temptation, that we may not be given up to the power of temptation. Our own hearts are the greatest tempters (James 1:14).[36]

We are in danger of Satan's temptations. Consider his malice in tempting. This hellish serpent is swelled with the poison of malice . . . To see a clod of dust so near to God, and himself [once a glorious angel] cast out of the heavenly paradise, makes him pursue mankind with inveterate hatred (Rev. 12:12). If there is anything this infernal spirit of hell can delight in, it is to ruin souls, and bring them into the same condemnation with himself.[37]

Consider Satan's diligence in tempting. He would have us idle, yet he himself is always busied (I Pet. 5:8), ever hunting after his prey.[38]

Consider Satan's power in tempting. He is "the prince of the world," "the strong man," and "the great red dragon," (John 12:31; Luke 11:21; Rev. 12:4). Satan has lost his holiness, but not his strength . . . He can blow the spark of lust into a flame . . . Consider his subtilty in tempting, using many policies to deceive . . . He is called a lion for his cruelty, and an old serpent for his subtilty . . . Satan tempts the ambitious man with a crown, the covetous man with a wedge of gold . . . He tempts when we have newly given up our name to Christ, when he finds us idle, when reduced to outward wants and straits, and after hearing the word, or prayer, or [celebrating] the sacrament.[39]

As the good Samaritan first had compassion on the wounded man—there was sympathy and then succour—so when we are wounded by the red dragon, Christ is first touched with compassion, and then he pours in wine and oil . . . Our Lord Jesus knows what it is to be tempted, therefore he is so ready to succour such as are tempted.[40]

We pray to be delivered from the evil of our own hearts, from the evil of Satan, from the evil of the world . . . that we may be kept from evil and make progress in piety (Titus 2:11, 12). We pray that God would deliver us more and more from the power and practice, from the scandalous acts of sin, which cast a reflection on the gospel.[41]

Sin is a breach of God's royal law, a contumacious affront to God, an act of high ingratitude, evil and foolish, polluting, debasing, enslaving, unsavoury, painful, defiling, disturbing . . . Thus you see what evil sin is, and why we need to pray, "Deliver us from evil."[42]

If you would be preserved from actual and scandalous sins, labour to mortify original sin, think what an odious thing sin is, get the fear of God planted in your hearts, be careful to avoid all the inlets and occasions of sin, study sobriety and temperance, watch your passions, consult with the oracles of God, be well-versed in Scripture (Ps. 119:11), get your hearts fired with love to God.[43]

We pray to be delivered from . . . the evil of our heart, the evil of Satan, the evil of the world. [But] abstaining from the external acts of sin is not sufficient to entitle us to salvation . . . We must make progress in holiness. Being divorced from sin is not enough, unless we are espoused to virtue. In Scripture these two are joined: "Depart from evil, and do good" (Ps. 34:14; Isa. 1:16) . . . Leaving sin is not enough, unless we embrace righteousness . . .

God delivered the three children out of the fiery furnace, Joseph out of prison, Daniel out of the lion's den . . . Let us then, in all our straits and exigencies, seek to God and say, "Deliver us from evil."[44]

FIVE

✖ JOHN OWEN ✖

1 6 1 6 — 8 3

A great systematic thinker devoted to the discovery of truth, its promotion of godliness, and termination in worship, John Owen has left subsequent generations a legacy of learned treatises on an impressive array of subjects. An Oxford man, committed to congregational views, defender of classical Calvinism over against Arminianism and Socinianism, Owen believed that the church should have no connection with the state and the state should not interfere in the affairs of the church. A friend of Oliver Cromwell's, sympathetic to the parliamentary cause, a leader in the Savoy Conference, he admired the preaching of Baxter and pleaded for Bunyan's release from prison. In 1662, he joined the ranks of the ejected. Among his voluminous and weighty writings are The Mortification of Sin in Believers (1656), Of Schism (1657), Temptation (1658), Discourse on the Holy Spirit (1674), Doctrine of Justification by Faith through the Imputation of the Righteousness of Christ (1677), and a seven-volume Commentary on the Epistle to the Hebrews (1668–84).

Discourse on the Holy Spirit

When God designed the great and glorious work of recovering fallen man and the saving of sinners, to the praise of the glory of his grace, he appointed, in his infinite wisdom, two great means thereof. The one was the giving of his Son for them, and the other was the giving of his Spirit unto them. And hereby was way made for the manifestation of the glory of the whole blessed Trinity; which is the utmost end of all the works of God. Hereby were the love, grace, and wisdom of the Father in the design and projection of the whole; the love, grace, and condescension of the Son in the execution, purchase, and procurement of grace and salvation for sinners; with the love, grace, and power of the Holy Spirit in the effectual application of all unto the souls of men, made gloriously conspicuous.[1]

When the Son of God was come, and had destroyed the works of the devil, the principal remaining promise of the New Testament, the spring of all the rest, concerns the sending of the Holy Spirit unto the accomplishment of his part of that great work which God had designed . . .

It is of great moment . . . that when our Lord Jesus Christ was to leave the world, he promised to send his Holy Spirit unto his disciples to supply his absence . . . This was the great legacy which our Lord Jesus Christ, departing out of this world, bequeathed unto his sorrowful disciples . . . The promise in general belongs unto all believers unto the end of the world.[2]

The great work of the Holy Ghost in the dispensation and ministration of the gospel . . . gives to the ministry of the gospel both its glory and its efficacy. Take away the Spirit from the gospel and you render it a dead letter, and leave the New Testament of no more use to Christians than the Old Testament is to the Jews . . .

There is not any spiritual or saving good from first to last communicated to us, or that we are from and by the grace of God made partakers of, but it is revealed to us and bestowed on us by the Holy Ghost . . . There is not anything done in us or by us that is holy and acceptable to God, but it is an effect of the Holy Spirit . . . Without him we can do nothing.[3]

By the Spirit alone is the grace of Christ communicated to us and wrought in us. By him we are *regenerated*; by him we are *sancti-*

fied; by him we are *cleansed*; by him we are *assisted* in, and unto every good work . . .

There are . . . many hurtful and noxious opinions concerning the Holy Ghost gone abroad in the world, and entertained by many, to the subversion of the faith which they have professed. Such as those whereby his deity and personality are denied . . .[4]

None can believe in Jesus Christ, or yield obedience to him, or worship God in him, but by the Holy Ghost. If the whole dispensation of the Spirit and his communications to the souls of men do cease, so does all faith in Christ, and Christianity also.[5]

It was the design of the Holy Ghost to give those whom he did extraordinarily inspire an assurance, sufficient to bear them out in the discharge of their duty, that they were acted on by himself alone; for in the pursuit of their work . . . they were to encounter various dangers, and some of them to lay down their lives for a testimony to the truth of the message delivered by them . . .[6]

The writing of the Scripture was another effect of the Holy Ghost, which had its beginning under the Old Testament . . . This ministry was first committed to Moses . . . who committed the will of God to writing.[7]

There is no good communicated to us from God but it is bestowed on us or wrought in us by the Holy Ghost. No gift, no grace, no mercy, no privilege, no consolation, do we receive, possess, or use, but it is wrought in us or manifested to us, by him alone. Nor is there any good in us towards God, any faith, love, duty, obedience, but what is effectually wrought in us by him, by him alone . . .[8]

The great work whereby God designed to glorify himself ultimately in this world was that of the *new creation*, or of the recovery and restoration of all things by Jesus Christ . . . The Holy Ghost does immediately work and effect whatever was to be done . . . for the perfecting and accomplishment of the Father's counsel and the Son's work.[9]

The framing, forming, and miraculous conception of the body of Christ in the womb of the blessed Virgin was the peculiar and especial work of the Holy Ghost . . . He was the wonderful *operator* in this glorious work.[10]

The human nature of Christ being thus formed . . . it was by the Holy Spirit positively endowed with all grace . . . with all those extraordinary powers and gifts which were necessary for the exercise and discharging of his office on the earth . . . kingly, sacerdotal, and prophetical . . . By him was he guided, directed, comforted, supported, in the whole course of his ministry, temptations, obedience, and sufferings.[11]

There was a peculiar work of the Holy Spirit in his [Christ's] resurrection, this being the completing act in laying the foundation of the church—the great testimony given to the finishing of the work of redemption . . . He was positively declared to be the Son of God by his resurrection from the dead, by the powerful working of the Holy Spirit.[12]

It was the Holy Spirit who glorified the human nature of Christ, and made it in every way fit for its eternal residence at the right hand of God, and a pattern for the glorification of the bodies of them that believe on him . . . He is the exemplar and pattern of that glory which in our mortal bodies we shall receive by the same Spirit.[13]

The Lord Christ had called his apostles to the great work of building his church, and the propagation of his gospel in the world. Of themselves, they were plainly and openly defective in all qualifications and abilities that might contribute anything to it. But whatever is wanting in themselves . . . he promises to supply . . . by sending the Holy Spirit to them, on whose presence and assistance alone depended the whole success of their ministry in the world . . . And this is the hinge whereon the whole weight of it turns and depends to this day. Take it away . . . and there will be an absolute end of the church of Christ in this world—no dispensation of the Spirit, no church.[14]

The Spirit represents the person of Jesus Christ. He works and effects whatever the Lord Christ had taken upon himself to work and effect towards his disciples . . . All their work and duty being suspended on the accomplishment of that promise, since he is God, they might suppose that he would come with some absolute new dispensation of truth, so that what they had learned and received from Christ should pass away and be of no use to them. To prevent any such apprehension, he lets them know that the work he had to do was only to carry on and build on the foundation which was laid in his person or doctrine. This was the Holy Spirit to do. And this he did.[15]

He who does not know that God has promised to "work in us" in a way of grace what he requires of us in a way of duty, has either never read the Bible or does not believe it, either never prayed or never taken notice of what he prayed for. He is a heathen and has nothing of the Christian in him, who does not pray that God would work in him what he requires of him. This we know: that what God commands and prescribes to us, what he encourages us to do, we ought with all diligence and earnestness [as we value our souls and their eternal welfare] to attend to and comply withal.[16]

A spiritual darkness and death came by sin on all mankind . . . In this state of things, the Holy Spirit undertook to create a new world . . . wherein righteousness should dwell. And this, in the first place, was by his effectual communication of a new principle of spiritual life to the souls of God's elect . . . This he does in their regeneration . . . All our faith and obedience to God, and all our acceptance with him, depend on our regeneration or being born again.[17]

He who cannot endure to *live to God* will as little endure to hear of being *born of God*.[18]

Regeneration consists in a spiritual renovation of our nature . . . This will infallibly produce a moral reformation of life.[19]

There is a work of God in us preceding all our good works towards him; for before we can work any of them, in order of nature, we must be the workmanship of God, created unto them, or enabled spiritually for the performance of them . . . The method of God's proceeding with us in his covenant is that he first washes and cleanses our natures, takes away the heart of stone, gives a heart of flesh, writes his law in our hearts, puts his Spirit in us. In this the grace of regeneration consists. The effect and consequence of this is that we shall walk in his statutes, keep his judgments and do them—that is, reform our lives, and yield all holy obedience to God.[20]

Unregenerate men . . . are spiritually dead. There is a necessity of an internal, powerful, effectual work of the Holy Ghost on the souls of men, to deliver them out of this state and condition by regeneration. And this principally respects their wills and affections, as the darkness and blindness before described relates to their minds and understandings. There is a spiritual life whereby men live unto God; to this they are strangers and aliens, and spiritually dead . . . The recovery and restoration of men by the grace of Christ is called their "quickening," or the bestowing of a new life upon them.[21]

The fountain of this life being in God, and the fulness of its being laid up in Christ for us, he communicates the power and principle of it to us by the Holy Ghost.[22]

The Holy Ghost is the immediate author and cause of the work of regeneration . . . Nothing is more in words acknowledged than that all the elect of God are sanctified by the Holy Ghost. And this regeneration is the head, fountain, or beginning of our sanctification, virtually comprising the whole in itself.[23]

God has appointed the ministry for the application of the word to the minds and consciences of men for their instruction and conversion . . . The word of God, thus dispensed by the ministry of the church is the only outward means used by the Holy Ghost in the regeneration of the adult to whom it is preached . . . It is sufficient to teach men all that is needful for them to believe and do, that they may be converted to God and yield him the obedience that he requires.[24]

No man ever circumcised his own heart. No man can say he began to do it by the power of his own will, and then God only helped him by his grace. As the act of outward circumcision on the body of a child was the act of another, and not of the child who was only passive therein [but the effect was in the body of the child only], so it is in the spiritual circumcision—it is the act of God, in which our hearts are the subject. It is the blindness, obstinacy, and stubbornness in sin that is in us by nature, with the prejudices which possess our minds and affections, which hinder us from conversion to God. But by the circumcision they are taken away.[25]

The God of peace . . . was in Christ reconciling the world to himself, destroying the enmity which entered in by sin, and laying the foundation of eternal peace. From hence it is that he will sanctify us, or make us holy . . . God, by the sanctification of our natures and persons, preserves that peace with himself in its exercize which he made and procured by the mediation of Christ . . . It is holiness that keeps up a sense of peace with God, and prevents those spiritual breaches which the remainders of our enmity would occasion. God, as the author of our peace, is the author of our holiness . . . by the Holy Ghost, the Spirit of love and peace.[26]

Sanctification . . . is the immediate work of God by his Spirit upon our whole nature, proceeding from the peace made for us by Jesus Christ, whereby, being changed into his likeness, we are kept entirely in peace with God, and are preserved unblamable, or in a state of gracious acceptation with him, according to the terms of the covenant, unto the end.[27]

Our principal duty in this world is to know aright what it is to be holy, and to be so indeed . . . There is in Scripture a twofold sanctification. The first is common to persons and things, consisting in . . . dedication, consecration, or separation to the service of God. But there is another kind of sanctification [consisting] in acts and duties of holy obedience to God.[28]

Holiness is not confined to this life, but passes over into *eternity* and glory. Death has no power over it, to destroy it or divest us of it . . . All those graces whereby holiness is constituted, and wherein it consists . . . shall in their present nature, improved to perfection, abide forever . . . That *love* whereby we now adhere to God as our chiefest good; that *faith* whereby we are united to Christ, our everlasting head; that *delight* in any of the ways or ordinances of God . . . that *love and good will* which we have for all those indwelt by the Spirit and bear the image of Christ . . . shall all be purified, enhanced, perfected, and pass into glory.[29]

Sanctification . . . is the universal renovation of our natures by the Holy Spirit into the image of God, through Jesus Christ.[30]

This work of *sanctification* differs from that of *regeneration* . . . Regeneration is instantaneous, consisting in one single creating act . . . But this work of sanctification is *progressive*, and admits of degrees.[31]

Among all the glorious works of God, next to that of redemption by Christ Jesus, my soul does most admire that of the Spirit in preserving the seed and principle of holiness in us, as a spark of living fire in the midst of the ocean, against all corruptions and temptations.[32]

A child who has a principle of life, a good natural constitution, and suitable food, will grow and thrive; but one who has obstructions from within, or distempers and disease, or falls and bruises, may be weak and thriftless. When we are regenerated, we are as new born babes, and ordinarily, if we have the sincere milk of the word we shall grow thereby. But if we give way to temptations, corruptions, negligences, conformity to the world, is it any wonder if we are lifeless and thriftless?

It is time for us rather to be casting off every weight and the sin that so easily besets us, to be by all means stirring up ourselves unto a vigorous recovery of our first faith and love, with an abundant growth in them . . . before our wounds become incurable.[33]

The spiritual beauty and comeliness of the soul consists in its conformity to God. Grace gives beauty . . . This beauty originally consisted in the image of God in us, which contained the whole order, harmony, and symmetry of our natures, in all their faculties and actions, with respect to God and our utmost end . . . Sin has a deformity in it, brings spots, stains, and wrinkles on the soul . . . Holiness and conformity to God is the honour of our souls. It is that alone which makes them truly noble . . . This we have only by holiness, or that image of God wherein we are created. Whatever is contrary to this is base, vile, and unworthy.[34]

We are purged and purified from sin by the Spirit of God . . . by the effectual working of the Holy Ghost in the rectifying and renovation of our natures.[35]

The Holy Ghost . . . gives a new understanding, a new heart, new affections, renewing the whole soul into the image of God . . . The most we have of saving light in our minds, of heavenly love in our wills and affections, of a constant readiness unto obedience in our hearts, the more pure we are, the more cleansed from the pollution of sin.[36]

The Holy Ghost purifies and cleanses us, by strengthening our souls by his grace unto all holy duties and against all natural sins . . . The blood of Christ immediately purges us from our sins by an especial application of it to our souls by the Holy Ghost, [who] proposes, declares, and presents to us the only true remedy, the only means of purification. To have a true spiritual sense of the defilement of sin, and a gracious view of the cleansing virtue of the blood of Christ is an eminent effect of the Spirit of grace.[37]

The Holy Spirit communicates the great, permanent, positive effect of holiness to the souls of believers and he guides and assists them in all the acts, works, and duties of holiness . . . Herein consists that image of God whereunto our natures are repaired by the grace of our Lord Jesus Christ, whereby we are made conformable unto God, firmly and steadfastly adhering to him through faith and love.[38]

There is a certain fixed rule and measure of this obedience, a conformity [to] the revealed will of God in the Scripture . . . The

secret will or hidden purposes of God are not the rule of our obedience, much less our own imaginations, inclinations, or reason . . .
But the Word of God is the adequate rule of all holy obedience.[39]

Have we received this principle of holiness and of spiritual life
by the gracious operation of the Holy Ghost? There are—among
many others—*three duties* incumbent on us, of which we ought to
be as careful as of our souls. First, carefully and diligently by all
means to cherish and preserve it in our hearts . . . Secondly, it is
equally incumbent on us to evince and manifest it by its fruits, in
the mortification of corrupt lusts and affections, in all duties of holiness, righteousness, charity, and piety in the world, that God may
be glorified . . . [Thirdly], in like manner it is required that we be
thankful for what we have received.

Without these visible fruits, we expose our entire profession of
holiness to reproach.[40]

All sanctified believers have an ability and power, in the renewed mind and understanding, to see, know, discern, and receive
spiritual things . . . the mysteries of the gospel, the mind of Christ—
in a due and spiritual manner. It is true, they have not all of them
this power and ability in the same degree; but every one of them has
enough of it to discern what concerns themselves and their duties
. . . Some of them seem, indeed, to be very low in knowledge . . .
And some of them are kept in that condition by their own negligence and sloth; they do not use as they ought . . . those means of
growing in grace and in the knowledge of Jesus Christ. But everyone who is truly sanctified, and who thereby has received the least
degree of saving grace, has light enough to understand the spiritual
things of the gospel in a spiritual manner.[41]

Salvation is the end that God aims at in his choosing of us, in
subordination to his own glory, which is and must be the ultimate
end of all his purposes and decrees, or of all the free acts of his wisdom and love. The means which he has ordained whereby we shall
be brought to this salvation, as designed in his eternal purpose, is
the sanctification of the Spirit. Gospel holiness, therefore, is the ef-

fect of that sanctification of the Spirit, which God has designed as the special way and means on their part of bringing the elect unto salvation; and his choosing of them is the cause and reason why he does so sanctify them by his Spirit.[42]

Seeing we are *chosen in Christ*, and predestinated to be like him, those graces of holiness have the most evident and legible characters of *electing love* upon them which are most effectual in working us unto a *conformity* to him. That grace is certainly from an eternal spring which makes us like Jesus Christ. Of this sort are meekness, humility, self-denial, contempt of the world, readiness to pass by wrongs, to forgive enemies, to love and do good to all—which indeed are despised by the most, and duly regarded but by few.[43]

All that is required of us, in the way of external obedience, is that our life style be such as becomes the gospel.[44]

Christ . . . is not only in himself, morally considered, the most perfect absolute, glorious, pattern of all grace, holiness, virtue, obedience to be chosen and preferred above all others, but he *alone* is so . . . One reason why God sent his Son to take our nature upon him, and to live in the world, was that he might set us an example in our own nature—in one who was like us in all things, sin only excepted—of that renovation of his image in us, of that return to him from sin and apostasy, of that holy obedience which he requires of us. Such an example was needful, that we might never be at a loss about the will of God in his commands with such a glorious representation of it before our eyes.[45]

To believe in Christ for redemption, for justification, for sanctification, is but one half of the duty of faith—it respects Christ only as he died and suffered for us, as he made atonement for our sins, peace with God, and reconciliation for us, as his righteousness is imputed to us for justification . . . We are exhorted to receive him and to believe in him, but this is not all that is required of us. Christ in the gospel is proposed to us as our pattern and example of holiness . . . Wherefore let us be much in the contemplation of what he was, what he did, how in all instances of duties and trials he carried himself, until an image or idea of his perfect holiness is implanted in our minds, and we are made like him thereby.[46]

Whereas the Spirit of God is everywhere said to *sanctify us*, we ourselves are commanded and said constantly to *mortify* our sins— the weakening, impairing, and destroying of the contrary principle of sin in its root and fruits.[47]

This duty of weakening sin by the growth and improvement of grace, and the opposition which is made to sin in all its actings, is called *mortification*, killing, or putting to death . . . By the entrance of grace into the soul [sin] loses its dominion, but not its being. The utter ruin, destruction, and gradual annihilation of all the remainders of this cursed life of sin is our design and aim in this work and duty.[48]

The Lord Christ calls all his true disciples to bear witness and testimony to the holiness of his life, the wisdom and purity of his doctrine, the efficacy of his death to expiate sin, to make atonement and peace with God, with the power of his whole mediation to renew the image of God in us, to restore us unto his favour, and to bring us to the enjoyment of him. This he calls all his disciples to avow unto and express in the world. By their so doing is he particularly glorified. A testimony is to be given unto and against the world, that his life was most holy, his doctrine most heavenly and pure, his death most precious and efficacious . . . All this is done in no other way than by obedience to him in holiness.[49]

SIX

❧ WILLIAM GOUGE ❧

1 5 7 8 — 1 6 5 3

Puritan and Presbyterian, William Gouge studied at Eton School and King's College, Cambridge. He lectured in logic and philosophy for several years, read fifteen chapters of the Bible daily, and observed the Sabbath scrupulously. From his ordination in 1608 to his death, he was associated with Blackfriar's Church in London. His preaching ministry attracted great crowds.

At the invitation of Parliament, he produced annotations on the Bible (I Kings to Job). Involved in the work of the Westminster Assembly from 1643, he participated in the preparation of its Confession of Faith. Among his published works are Domestical Duties *(1622),* The Whole Armour of God *(1627),* An Explanation of the Lord's Prayer *(1626),* God's Three Arrows *(1631),* The Saint's Sacrifice *(1632), and a massive expository* Commentary on Hebrews *(1655).*

Domestic Duties

As there are two vocations to which it has pleased God to call everyone—one *general,* by virtue of which certain common duties are required to be performed by all [such as knowledge, faith, obedience, repentance, love, mercy, justice, truth, etc.], the other *particular,* by virtue of which certain specific duties are required of several persons, according to those distinct places wherein the Divine Providence has set them in the Commonwealth, Church, or family, so ought God's ministers to be careful in instructing God's people in both kinds of duties—both those which concern their *general* and those also which concern their *particular* calling.[1]

It is the duty of Christians to set forth the praise of God and to be serviceable to one another. For this purpose in the Decalogue, to the first table which prescribes the duty we owe to God, is added the second table which declares the service that we owe to one another.

The service which in the fear of God we perform one to another, is an evident and real demonstration of the respect we bear to God . . . This discovers the hypocrisy of those who make great pretence of praising God, and yet are scornful and disdainful to their brothers, and slothful to do any service to mankind . . . Surely the outward service they pretend to perform to God does not so much wipe out the spot of profanity as their neglect of duty to man brands their foreheads with the stamp of hypocrisy.[2]

It is a general mutual duty appertaining to all Christians, to submit themselves to one another. The magistrate, by ruling with meekness and humility, submits himself to his subject . . . The reason why all are bound to submit themselves one to another is because every one is set in his place by God, not so much for himself, as for the good of others . . . Let every one, therefore, high and low, rich and poor, superior and inferior, magistrate and subject, minister and people, husband and wife, parent and child, master and servant, neighbours and fellows, all of all sorts in their several places take notice of this duty . . . and make conscience to put it in practice.[3]

The fear of God is an aweful respect of the divine Majesty. Sometimes it arises from faith in the mercy and goodness of God. When the heart of man has once felt a sweet taste of God's goodness, and found that in his favour alone all happiness consists, it is stricken with such an inward awe and reverence as it would not for anything displease his Majesty, but rather do whatsoever it may know to be pleasing and acceptable to him.

There are two effects which arise from this kind of godly fear: a careful endeavour to please God . . . a careful avoiding of such things as offend the Majesty of God and grieve his Spirit.[4]

No submission is be performed unto man, but that which may stand with the fear of God . . . Great reason is there that all service should be limited by the fear of God, for God is the highest Lord to whom all service is primarily and principally due. Whatsoever service is due to any man, high or low, it is due in and for the Lord . . . Besides, God is that great judge to whom all of all sorts, superiors and inferiors, are to give an account of their service.[5]

The family is a seminary of the Church and Commonwealth. It is like a bee hive, in which is the stock and out of which are sent many swarms of bees. In families are all sorts of people bred and brought up, and out of families are they sent into the Church and Commonwealth . . . A family is a little Church, and a little Commonwealth . . . whereby trial may be made of such as are fit for any place of authority . . . It is a school wherein the first principles and grounds of government and submission are learned.[6]

The title "head" is given to Christ in two respects: in regard of his dignity and dominion over the Church, and in regard to the close union between him and the Church . . . Much comfort and great confidence must this minister to all such as have assurance of belonging to this body. For having so mighty, so wise, so merciful a head . . . so sufficient in every way, who can instruct, direct, guide, govern, protect, and help them in all their needs whatsoever. Why should they be afraid?

Oh how happy a thing is it for the Church that it has such a head! A head that does not tyrannize over it, nor trample it under foot . . . but procures peace and safety for it.[7]

Christ is a most absolute and perfect Saviour. He is in every way a sufficient Saviour, able to save perfectly even to the very uttermost. He saves soul and body. He saves from all manner of misery . . . Sin is the greatest and most grievous evil, indeed, the cause of all misery. Those who are saved from it are saved from all evil.

In that Christ saves from sin, he saves from the wrath of God, the curse of the law, the venom of all outward crosses, the tyranny of Satan, the sting of death, the power of the grave, the torments of hell . . .[8]

Christ is the only Saviour of man . . . None is able, none is worthy, to work so great a work. Jesus must do it, or it cannot be done. But he is so able, and so worthy, that he can do it of himself and needs none to assist him . . . Let us, for our part, turn to this Saviour alone, and wholly rely on him since we desire to be saved. So shall we honour him, by preferring him before all—yes, by rejecting all but him. Thus shall we be sure to bring help, ease, and comfort to our own souls.[9]

All who are once incorporated into Christ shall be saved. The body comprises not only arms, shoulders, breast, back, and such like, but also hands, fingers, feet, toes and all. Christ their head being their Saviour, who can doubt of their salvation?

Adam conveys sin and death to all who descend from him . . . Christ conveys grace and life to every one who is given to him . . . This is a point of admirable comfort to such as have assurance of their incorporation into Christ, since they may rest upon the benefit of the office of Christ, that he is a Saviour.[10]

So long as men remain destitute of the Spirit of Christ, and are possessed of a contrary spirit, they may well be judged for the present to be none of his body, nor to have any part in Christ. Their future estate, however, is referred to him who only knows what it shall be.

The extent of the Church's subjection to Christ is unlimited . . . For there is nothing which Christ requires of her, but that she may with a good conscience—and must in obedience—accept. Just, pure, and perfect are all his commandments. There is no error in any of them. No mischief or unseemliness can follow upon the keeping of them.[11]

None but the upright, who are indeed renewed by the sanctifying Spirit of Christ, will in all things make Christ's will their rule and in everything hold close to it, preferring it before their pleasure, profit, preferment, or any other outward allurement. They who do so give good evidence that they belong to the body of Christ, and may be sure that Christ is their Saviour.

Christ became a King to govern us, a Prophet to instruct us, a Priest to make atonement for us . . . He wholly set himself apart for our use and benefit.[12]

Learn to consider Christ's death, not as the death of a private man, but of a public person—of a surety, of a pledge—that in our place and stead was made sin, and was made a curse, to redeem us from our sins and from the curse which had fallen upon us on account of sin. The comfort and benefit of Christ's death is lost if this be not known and believed. In this consists a main difference between the death of Christ and all other men—not even the most righteous martyrs excepted. Their death was but a duty . . . no ransom, as Christ's was.[13]

The price of our redemption is of infinite value. Neither Christ nor God himself could give a greater. Heaven and earth and all things in them are not of like worth . . .

What place can be left for despair in those who know and believe the worth of this ransom? What can be held too dear for him—can goods, friends, children, liberty, life, anything else?

How ungrateful, how unworthy of Christ are they who for his sake will not forsake their transient honours, fading wealth, vain pleasures, garrish attire, and such like trash?[14]

Christ in his death aimed at our good. He was made sin for us, that we might be made the righteousness of God in him . . . This proves Christ's giving of himself to be a fruit of his love . . . Let us learn to apply all that Christ did to ourselves . . . Let us also learn how to manifest love—namely, by seeking and procuring the good of others . . . If this were practised, would there be such oppressing, such undermining, such deceiving, such wronging of one another as there is?

Let that mind be in us which was in Christ Jesus, and thus manifest our love . . .[15]

Christ seeks the purity of his Church. For this end has he shed his own most precious blood and conveyed his Holy Spirit into his body, the Church. Cleansing and sanctifying do more distinctly set forth the purity of the Church, even in this world. *Cleansing* has reference to the blood of Christ and so points to our justification. *Sanctifying* has reference to the Spirit of Christ, who works our sanctification.

The guilt of sin by Christ's death is clean taken away . . . because it is not imputed to us . . . The Church is made holy by that inherent righteousness which the Spirit of Christ works in all the members of his body.[16]

It is the course of a man's life, not this or that particular action, which makes a man blameworthy or blameless—just as the flock of swallows, and not one here or another there makes it springtime. Now because the constant bearing of those who are of the Church is before men blameless, they may justly be so accounted, notwithstanding some particular things blameworthy do sometimes come from them . . . True saints may boldly lift up their faces before God and man. The soundness of their faith produces confidence before God. The testimony of their conscience produces courage before men. Let all who desire this boldness join a sound faith and a good conscience together and labour for assurance of their cleansing by the blood of Christ, and sanctifying by the Spirit of Christ.[17]

Justification goes before sanctification . . . The grace of justification is a most free grace. It is not wrought upon any righteousness of ours, but it is before it . . . Let none, therefore, boast of their cleansing by Christ's blood till they find themselves renewed and sanctified by the Spirit of Christ . . . To whom is there no condemnation? To them that are in Christ Jesus. Who are they? They who walk not after the flesh, but after the Spirit. Sanctification presupposes justification . . . Sanctification is a fruit of justification.

Admirable is the comfort which the saints in this world reap hereby . . . Since their sanctification is a fruit and evidence of their justification, they take heart . . . Thus upheld and comforted, they continue to strive against sin till it be clean rooted out of them as well as remitted.[18]

There is a double loving of a man's self. One good and commendable, the other evil and damnable. Spiritual self-love is supernaturally wrought in man by God's Spirit, so that he is both enlightened to discern what is most excellent and best for him, and also moved to choose the same . . . Hence it comes to pass that their chiefest care is for their souls and for their eternal salvation.[19]

Self-love is evil when it is cast upon our corruptions, our lusts, our evil humours, when we affect and love them, and for them pursue whatsoever may satisfy them . . .

Evil self-love is a most detestable vice, but it is both lawful and commendable to love one's self aright.[20]

It is especially noted of Christ, that as there was occasion he slept, he ate, he rested and otherwise refreshed himself . . . Against this good instinct of nature do many offend. Covetous misers, who so dote upon their wealth and so delight in abundance of goods treasured up, that they afford not themselves things needful to nourish their bodies . . . Such men make their riches to be snares and hindrances, to keep them from eternal life . . . Others are too intent upon their businesses, even the affairs of their lawful callings . . . In this, many students, preachers, lawyers, tradesmen, farmers, labourers, and others offend [for in good things there may be excess] . . . They who by such means disable themselves make themselves guilty of the neglect of so much good as they might have done, if they had nourished and cherished their bodies.[21]

The Lord nourishes and cherishes his Church . . . When he first created man, he provided beforehand all things needful to nourish him . . . When he was moved to destroy the earth . . . he had care of his Church and provided an ark to keep her out of the water and stored up in the ark all things needful for her. When he purposed to bring a famine on the world, he sent a man beforehand to lay up provision for his Church. When his Church was in a barren and dry wilderness, he gave them bread from heaven, water out of the rock . . . After this he brought his Church into a land flowing with milk and honey . . . Neither has he merely nourished her with temporal blessings, but also with all needful spiritual blessings—his word and sacraments, his Spirit and grace . . . With his own flesh and blood has he fed her, and with his own righteousness has he clothed her.[22]

The privilege which the saints receive by their union with Christ in the time of death [that time from their departure out of this world till the general resurrection] is admirable. For when the body and soul are severed from one another, neither soul nor body are separated from Christ. Both remain united to him, just as when Christ's body and soul were by death severed from one another, neither his soul nor his body were separated from the Deity but both remained united to it. This inviolable bond that holds the saints united to Christ in death is the benefit of a spiritual union . . . The bodies of the saints are preserved to enjoy eternal glory together with their souls, but the bodies of the wicked are reserved . . . to appear at the bar of God's judgment seat, and there receive the sentence of condemnation.[23]

The mystery of our union with Christ is a matter of great comfort and encouragement . . . It is also a matter of direction and instigation to us for the performing of sundry duties . . . Some of the most principal are these: *Confidence* in Christ . . . our head, so mighty, wise, tender . . . *Subjection* answerable to his manner of governing us . . . willingly and readily . . . *Cleansing* our souls from all filthiness of flesh and spirit . . . *Conformity* to the image of Christ in true holiness and righteousness . . . *Heavenly affections* . . . where our head is, there also ought our heart to be . . . *Courage against death*. Seeing that in death we are Christ's, what cause have we to fear death?[24]

The union between Christ and the Church is a great mystery . . . Let us not presume to measure it with the line of our own reason. It being a great mystery, it is above our capacity. Yet, because it is revealed we must believe it, as we do the mysteries of the Trinity, of Christ's eternal generation, of the personal union of his two natures, of the proceeding of the Holy Ghost . . . because the word has revealed them . . . Here we must believe what we know but in part; there, we shall perfectly know whatsoever is to be believed. Preachers can but in part make known this mystery, and hearers can but in part conceive it. Let us, therefore, wait for perfect under-standing of it . . . but meantime believe without doubting that which is revealed . . .[25]

The ends for which marriage was ordained . . . are especially three. First, that the world might be increased . . . with a legitimate brood and distinct families which are the seminaries of cities and commonwealths; also that in the world the Church might be pre-served and propagated by an holy seed. Second, that men might avoid fornication . . . Against this hereditary disease no remedy is so effective as this . . . For those that have not the gift of conti-nence, this is the only warranted and sanctified remedy . . . Third, that man and wife might be a mutual help to one another . . . in health and sickness.[26]

St. Peter requires such a bearing of man and wife one towards another that their prayers be not hindered. He takes it for granted that prayer is a mutual duty which one owes to the other. In this may man and wife be helpful to each other in all things needful to either of them . . . By many it is counted a slight duty and of small use. But the truth is that to perform it aright . . . is both difficult in the deed and powerful in the effect. It is the best duty that one can perform for another, and the least to be neglected.[27]

After the good of the soul, follows the good of the body, wherein husband and wife must show their provident care of each other, and do what lies in them to procure the welfare of another's person . . . This duty extends itself to all estates of prosperity and adversity, of health and sickness, even as they mutually covenant and promise when they are first joined in marriage . . . Wherefore they ought both to rejoice in the welfare of one another, and also in all distress to succour and comfort each other, putting their shoulders under one another's burden, and helping to ease one another as much as they can.[28]

That love which naturally parents bear to their children ought in equity to breed in children a love to their parents. For love deserves love, and most unworthy are they to be loved who cannot love in return. The love of parents above all others is to be answered with love on the children's part, to the uttermost of their power, because it is free, great, and constant.

Besides, there is a necessity of love in children to their parents, lest for lack thereof, their subjection (which above all ought to be most free) should turn into slavish servitude.[29]

If parents have been persons of good bearing in their lifetime, as religious towards God, just in their dealings with man, merciful to such as stood in need of their help, doing much good in their place, and so ended their days with much credit, it is an especial means to maintain and continue their credit, for children to walk in their steps and endeavour to be like them.

Thus is a blessed memory of their parents kept fresh and green though their bodies be rotten. For when they who knew the parents behold the like good qualities and actions in their children, they will be put in mind of the parties deceased and say, Oh how such parents yet live! Behold a lively and living image of them![30]

Piety is the best thing that a parent can teach a child, for as reason makes a man differ from a beast, and as learning and civility make a wise and sober man differ from savages and swaggerers, so piety makes a sound Christian much more to differ from the most civil and well ordered natural man that can be. Learning, civility, calling, portion, are all nothing without piety . . .

There is a necessity that children be taught piety, because they are not born but made Christians . . . Parents are by God made watchmen over their children . . . They must therefore nurture them in the admonition of the Lord.[31]

SEVEN

✻ HENRY SMITH ✻

1 5 5 0 — 9 1

---

*Early influenced by the Puritan Richard Greenham, Henry Smith devel-
oped into a "silver-tongued preacher . . . the prime preacher of the nation."*[1]

*He was gifted with a phenomenal memory and amazing for pulpit
eloquence. Yet his preaching was plain and powerful rather than ornate.
Smith sought to further the reformation process within the Church of
England. His ministry at fashionable St. Clement Danes in London emphasized the need of validating a profession of faith by the practical pursuit of holiness.*

*When illness limited his pulpit ministry, Smith gave increased at-
tention to writing and publishing. The printing of sermons was apparently
big business in Elizabethan England. Taken down by short hand tran-
scription, sermons were printed and sold. Several versions often ap-
peared, occasioning controversy between stenographers and printers, as
well as authors and authorities. From 1589 to 1610, there were no fewer
than 83 printings of Smith's sermons. Here are some of the titles:* A
Preparative to Marriage, An Examination of Usury, The Pride, Fall
and Restitution of Nebuchadnezzar, The Honour of Humility, The
Art of Hearing, Noah's Drunkenness, Jacob's Ladder, *and* The Benefit of Contentation.

*Smith's name on a sermon was "so attractive to buyers that it was
charged that unscrupulous printers forged sermons over his name when
they could not lay their hands upon authentic copy."*[2]

*Excerpts from several of his printed sermons (*The Art of Hearing,
The Humility of Paul, Food for New-born Babes, A Caveat for

Christians, *The Poor Man's Tears, The Trial of the Righteous, The Pilgrim's Wish, The Godly Man's Request, The Ladder of Peace, The True Trial of the Spirits, and* The Benefit of Contentation) *will give us some idea of his exposition and application.*

An age that seems to have lost its taste for the plain proclamation of the Word may dismiss much Puritan preaching as ponderous and consider Smith's sermons as dull. Yet the examples we possess of his pulpit ministry show him to be serious about making God's Word plain through straightforward explanation of the biblical text and interesting comparisons and contrasts drawn from the Scriptures or the daily experiences of his contemporaries.

The Art of Hearing
Luke 8:18

Take heed how you hear. This is the warning of Christ to his disciples, after they had heard the parable of the seed (Luke 8:18) . . . When I consider how many labourers God has sent to his vineyard, and yet how little fruit it yields to the sower, I cannot impute it to the lack of teaching, but to the lack of hearing . . . to a kind of negligent hearing [so that] a thousand sermons have been lost and forgotten, as though they had never been preached at all.

The devil . . . labours all that he can to keep us from hearing. To effect this, he keeps us at taverns, at plays, in our shops . . . He casts fancies into our minds, drowsiness into our heads, sounds into our ears, temptations before our eyes . . . He infects us with prejudice of the preacher . . . or takes us to dinner, or pastime, to remove our minds, that we should think no more of it.[3]

The devil . . . also has this trick: instead of applying the doctrine, which we should follow, he turns us to praise and extol the preacher . . . Take heed how you hear . . . There is nothing so easy as to hear, and yet there is nothing so hard as to hear well.[4]

Observe five things: the necessity of hearing; the fruit which comes by hearing; the kinds of hearers; the danger of hearing amiss; the manner of hearing which will make you remember what is said, and teach you more in a year than you have learned all your life.[5]

Christ calls none to him; but them which hunger and thirst, as if none were fit to hear the Word, but they which hunger after it and bring a stomach with them.[6]

In Exodus 3:5, God teaches us how to hear when he speaks to Moses and bids him put off his shoes. So should we put off our lusts, thoughts, cares, fancies, and all our business, when God speaks . . . In I Cor. 6:1, Paul teaches us how to hear when he says, "Receive not the grace of God in vain," showing that many hear comfort, and are not comforted; many hear instruction, and are not instructed. James teaches us how to hear (1:22) when he says, "Be not hearers only, but doers," showing that you should do as you hear . . . In Luke 10, Mary teaches us how to hear, when she leaves all to sit at Christ's feet and mark his doctrine. In Luke 2, the Virgin teaches us how to hear. When she heard the sayings of Anna, Simeon, and Christ, it is said that she pondered them and treasured them up in her heart—showing that our ears should be but messengers to the heart.[7]

If you hear comfort, apply that to fear; if you hear a promise, apply that to your distrust; if you hear a threatening, apply that to your presumption; and fill up the gap where the devil would enter.[8]

Think that the Word is an epistle from God . . . the will wherein legacies are written, a charge from the Judge of life and death.

Two things out of every sermon are especially to be noted: that which you did not know before, and that which speaks to your own sin. So shall you increase your knowledge, and lessen your vices.[9]

Think that you are gathering manna, and that it is God who speaks to you, and that you shall give account for every lesson you hear.[10]

The Humility of Paul
Romans 12:1, 2

Paul, an apostle to the Gentiles, writing to the Romans, showed them what God had done for them. Now he shows them what they should do for God . . . That is, as Christ gave himself for you, so you must now give yourselves to him. As he was sacrificed for you, so you must be sacrificed for him. Not your sheep, not your oxen, nor your goats, but yourselves. You must be the sacrifice—living, holy, and acceptable.[11]

It was Paul's office to teach the Romans, but his policy to beseech the Romans. Paul humbled himself to his inferiors, to make them humble themselves to God . . . God is love, and his ministers must speak like love, or else they do not speak like Paul. Whoever fishes for souls, and does not take this net, shall fish all day in vain.[12]

There is a plurality of God's mercies . . . his temporal mercies on earth, and his everlasting mercies in heaven . . . So we are to give our bodies a sacrifice to God . . . Every member owes a duty to the Creator: the heart to love him, the hand to serve him, the tongue to praise him, the ear to hear him, the foot to follow him.[13]

The devil is called the god of this world, because the world's fashions are the devil's fashions . . . To jump with the world is to leap to hell . . . Sanctification begins within. Until the mind be renewed, the body is never sacrificed.[14]

Scripture calls for a new man, a new creature, a new heart. David asks the Lord to create in him a new heart, not to correct his old heart . . . showing that his heart was like an old garment, so rotten and tattered that he could make no good of it by patching or piercing (Ps. 51:10) . . . Therefore Paul says, Cast off the old man. Not, pick and wash him till he be clean, but cast him off and begin anew, as David did. Would you know what this renewing is? It is restoring the image of God, until we be like Adam when he dwelt in Paradise.[15]

Food for New-born Babes
I Peter 2:2

First Peter 2:2 contains an exhortation to incite and stir up the believing Jews. As God had enlightened them with some knowledge of his truth and sanctified them in some measure with the grace of his Spirit, so they should proceed . . . and daily increase more and more in the faith and fear of Jesus Christ.[16]

Now the means whereby we receive all our growth and increase in God is the lively preaching of the Word of truth . . . Therefore thirst and long for the Word of God as little infants [which are new born] cry for the mother's milk to nourish and sustain them . . . God is our Father to beget us; the Church, his spouse, our Mother to conceive us; the seed whereby we are bred and born again is the Word of God; the nurses to feed and wean and cherish us are the ministers of the gospel; and the food whereby we are nourished and held in life is the milk of the Word.[17]

All who would profit in the school of Christ, and receive light and comfort by the preaching of the Word, are here taught to become as "babes," to lay aside all malice, and bring holy and sanctified hearts to the hearing of it.[18]

We must not be children in wavering and inconstancy . . . carried about with every wind of doctrine . . . like a drunken man from wall to wall (Eph. 4:14; I Cor. 14:20) . . . But we must be children in an ardent affection, in thirsting and longing for the Word of God . . . Our faith is not able to sustain and support itself, unless it be presently nourished with the food of life . . . "Let the Word of God dwell in you" (Col. 3:16), because it must not take up a night's lodging and be gone, but must have a continual residence and abode in our hearts.[19]

If we be Christians [let us] persevere, and take heed lest we fall . . . Not, lest we fall from our election, but lest we fall from our righteousness . . . We must have confidence towards God, but diffidence towards ourselves.[20]

The Israelites fell . . . they flitted from sin to sin, like a fly which shifts from sore to sore. They tempted the Lord, murmured, lusted, committed idolatry, [and] served the flesh . . . As they fell away, so may you. But by their fall, you may also learn to stand.

Who can say what he will do when he is tried?

The best men have had their slips, but always they rose again—as though they had sinned to teach us repentance . . . Therefore, their sins are written . . . to admonish us . . . We must behold the sins of others, to learn by them . . . These things are not written for our imitation, but for our admonition.[21]

Strong men have fallen—Solomon, David, Noah, Lot, Samson, Peter—tall cedars, strong oaks, fair pillars, lie in the dust. Can I look upon these ruins without compassion, or remember them without fear, unless I be a reprobate, and my heart of flint?[22]

Am I stronger than Samson, wiser than Solomon, chaster than David, soberer than Noah, firmer than Peter, if God should leave me to myself, if he should withdraw his hand which holds me?

This is a memorandum to all, so especially let him that rules, and him that teaches, take heed lest he fall, for if the pillars shrink, the temple shakes . . . Let them which are down care to rise, and the Lord so direct our steps, that we may rise again.[23]

The Poor Man's Tears
Matthew 10:42

I know that in these days and in this iron age it is as hard a thing to persuade men to part with money as to pull out their eyes and cast them away . . . Nevertheless, I cannot but wonder that men are so slow in giving of alms and so hard-hearted towards the relief of the poor, when the promises of God warrant them not to lose their reward . . . The kingdom of heaven belongs to him that shelters strangers, clothes the naked, feeds the hungry, comforts the sick, and performs such charitable acts of compassion (I John 3:17; Matt. 25: 31–46) . . . The excellency of Christians consists in leading a godly life, and giving of alms . . . a charitable relief given to the sick, the lame, the blind, the powerless, the needy, the hungry [out of] that which God has mercifully bestowed upon us.[24]

As to teaching how much we should give, we are taught that if we have much we should give accordingly; if we have but little, give what we can spare . . . The tears of men, women, and children, are grievous and pitiful; and tears give cause of great compassion, especially the tears of such as are constrained to beg for their relief . . . I therefore exhort you by the lamentable tears which the poor do daily shed through hunger and extreme misery to be good, charitable, and merciful to them.[25]

Such as hoard up wealth and have no regard to the relief of the poor [will find their wealth at death] to melt and consume away like butter in the sun . . . Learn to forsake the covetous world, before it forsake you . . . Leave wishing, and fall to some doing.[26]

If the proud would leave their superfluity in apparel . . . the greater part would suffice towards the relief of the poor . . . Let the glutton seek only to suffice nature and leave his daily surfeiting in belly-cheer . . . Let the whoremonger leave off his dalliance and inordinate expenses for the maintaining of his wickedness . . . Let every tradesman live orderly, not spending money vainly at dice— but live as becomes civil Christians in the fear of God, they may have sufficient for the maintenance of themselves and their family, and yet the poor may be by them sufficiently relieved.[27]

The Trial of the Righteous
Psalm 34:19

As the eyelid is made to open and shut, to save the eye, so patience is set to keep the soul and save the heart whole, to cheer the body again. Therefore if you note when you can go by an offence and take a little wrong, and suffer trouble quietly, you have a kind of peace and joy in your heart, as if you had gotten a victory. The greater is your patience, the less is your pain . . . "In all things" says

Paul, "we are more than conquerors" (Rom. 8:37) . . . As the tree
which Moses cast into the spring seasoned the bitterness of the waters, so patience cast into our troubles, seasons the bitterness of the
cross . . . This power has God given to patience, the medicinable
virtue, that it should be like a wholesome herb in the world, or a
general physician for all persons and diseases.[28]

A man's wisdom is known by his patience [endurance], as though
the impatient cannot be wise. By patience we receive the promises
. . . Patience breeds experience, and experience hope, as though he
who lacks patience has no experience of God, to know the scope of his
doings, nor any hope to comfort him about the life to come . . . If we
suffer with Christ, we shall reign with Christ . . . The Lord loves those
he chastens, and by suffering we are made like the Son of God.

By patience Job did bear all the torments that the devil could
heap upon him; by patience Joseph forgave his brothers, when he
might have put them to death . . . by patience Christ suffered ban-
ishment, reproaches, and scourges, until he went to death, like a
lamb to the slaughter.[29]

Although the troubles of the righteous are many, the Lord de-
livers him out of them all . . . There are two things which make us
take our troubles grievously: one, because we do not expect them before they come . . . second, we are like the prophet's servant who saw
his foes but not his friends (I Kings 6). So we see our sore, but not
our salve . . . Therefore we go about to deliver ourselves, as though
we could . . . Bear both these sentences in mind, that you must go
through a sea of troubles, and then you shall come to the haven of
rest, and no affliction shall take you before you be armed for it, and
in every trouble you shall know where to find your remedy.[30]

This is the state of the Church militant; she is like the ark,
floating upon the waters, like a lily growing among thorns, like the
bush which burned with fire but was not consumed; so the city of
God is always besieged; but never ruined. Christians and persecu-
tions [are] close together, like Christ and his cross . . . Their peace
in persecution, their rest labour, their riches poverty, their glory re-

proaches, their liberty imprisonment . . . [like stones] they must be squared for the temple [by] a generation of crosses, and a plurality of troubles . . . All this while Christ seemed to sleep, as he did in the ship. Now he rebukes the winds and waves, and troubles fly before him . . . the Sun rose, and the mists vanished.[31]

The Pilgrim's Wish
Philippians 1:23

Here is Paul's desire, to be dissolved. Why? That he might be with Christ . . . The faithful long to go to Christ. For unless we ascend to him, as he descended to us, his descending is in vain because he came down that we might go up . . . He descended to be crucified, we ascend to be glorified . . . Good cause had Paul to desire to be with Christ. Yet he will not dissolve himself, but desires to be dissolved . . . neither does he make any petition to God to take away his life . . . Paul would have us learn that death is better than life because it leads to Christ . . . The faithful rejoice that they shall go to Christ . . . This is our glory and life, that he lives in glory . . . If the head be crowned, all the body is more honoured . . . Where the head is, there the body must needs be.[32]

Paul calls his death not a destruction, but a dissolution . . . he departs from this life . . . his soul departs from the body until the day of resurrection . . . he departs from this vale of misery into the paradise of joy and all felicity, to live and reign with God for ever.

Death is the way to Christ, [not] purgatory . . . the most profitable lie in all popery . . . We must go to Abraham's bosom or hell fire. There are but two kinds of men, and therefore but two ways. Where then is purgatory, which the best of the Fathers confesses that he could never find in Scripture?[33]

Much have they to answer, which are not contented to die in peace, and stay till they be dissolved, but [act] as though they were the authors of life and death . . . to cast asunder that which God has joined: the loving soul and their body.[34]

The Godly Man's Request
Psalm 90:12

Moses prays for himself and the rest: "Teach us, O Lord, to number our days, that we may apply our hearts to wisdom." That is, seeing we must needs die, teach us to think of our death that we may die in your fear, to live again. The consideration of our mortality will make us apply our hearts to godliness.

This is the day of salvation . . . Work out your salvation. This is a long task. Therefore we need to number our days and not lose a minute, lest we be benighted before our work is done . . . Else we cannot "apply our hearts to wisdom." Unless we think upon death, we cannot fashion ourselves to a godly life. [We] must pray, fast, watch, hear, and do, as becomes him who shall shortly give account of his stewardship.[35]

There is no such enemy to repentance as to think that we have time enough to repent hereafter . . . But "he died" is the epitaph of every man . . . Every man is a tenant at will, and there is nothing sure in life but death . . . The rich glutton is locked in his grave as firmly as poor Lazarus (Luke 16:22) . . . This is the last bed which every man shall sleep in . . . All of us are born one way, and die a hundred ways.[36]

Our life is but a short life . . . For one apple that falls from the tree, ten are pulled before they are ripe, and the parents mourn for the death of their children as often as the children for the decease of their parents . . . Watch, because you know not when the Lord will come to take you, or to judge you.[37]

The Ladder of Peace
I Thessalonians 5:16–18

The Apostle commends to us three virtues of greater price than the three presents which the wise men brought to Christ. The first is, "Rejoice evermore." The second is, "Pray continually." The third is,

"In all things give thanks . . ." These are the three things which all men do and no man does as he should.[38]

This may well be called The Ladder of Peace, for it stands upon three steps, and every step is a step from trouble to peace, from sorrow to joys, and he who can give thanks has obtained his desire. A man cannot rejoice, and mourn; cannot pray, and despair; cannot give thanks, and be offended . . . When you forget to rejoice in the Lord, then you begin to muse, to fear, to distrust, and at last to despair, and then every thought seems to be a sin against the Holy Ghost.[39]

How many sins does the afflicted conscience record against itself, repenting for breaking this commandment, and that commandment, and never repent for breaking this commandment: "Rejoice ever more"?

The Son of God is called "the consolation of Israel," to show that he brings consolation with him, and that joy is where Christ is, as light is where the sun is. The chiefest joy is called "the joy of the Holy Ghost," to show that those who have the chiefest joy have the Holy Ghost . . . The greatest peace is called "the peace of conscience," to show that they have the greatest peace who have a good conscience.[40]

As God loves "a cheerful giver," so he loves a cheerful server, and a cheerful preacher, and a cheerful hearer, and a cheerful worshipper . . . God requires no sorrow but the sorrow for sins; no fear but the fear to sin; no care, but the care to please him.[41]

Pray continually . . . When the heart rejoices in God, then is it fittest to call upon God . . . The godly have another joy which the world knows not of. "A good conscience is a continual feast" (Prov. 15:5).[42]

If we cannot rejoice in praying, how shall we rejoice in suffering? No man has such joy as he that is often talking with God in prayer . . . for the company of God is nothing but joy, and gladness of heart. [43]

When we read, God speaks to us, because we read his Word. But when we pray, we speak to God . . . "The prayers of the saints" are called "incense" because when they ascend to heaven God seems to smell a sweet savour like incense.

Who ever fell into heresy, or into apostasy, or into despair, before he fell from prayer, the preservative of the soul? If prayer had been here, these evils had not happened. This is the "holy water" which drives away unclean spirits (Matt. 17:21) . . . It is a good thing to preach, and yet you see we do not presume to preach before we pray, because Paul plants, Apollos waters, but *God* gives the increase.[44]

We are not commanded to preach, hear, fast, watch, or give continually. But we are commanded to pray continually, as though prayer were more needful than all the rest . . . We lack continually, and we are tempted continually, and we sin continually. Therefore, we need to pray to God continually, that God would supply our wants and forgive our sins, and prevent our temptations.

To pray continually is to lift up our hearts continually to God, and to pray in our thoughts. . . . though we open not our lips.[45]

God is readier to give, than we to ask. Therefore let us pray that our neglect of prayer may be forgiven.[46]

The True Trial of the Spirits
I Thessalonians 5:19–22

"Quench not the Spirit. Despise not prophesying. Try all things and keep that which is good. Abstain from all appearance of evil."

Zeal is the fire of the Spirit . . . God is pleased with zeal as men are pleased with love . . . Our goal should be a temperate zeal . . . The disciples were commended for their zeal when they left all to follow Christ. But Christ reproved them for their zeal when they would pray for fire from heaven to consume the Samaritans.[47]

All do not prophesy alike . . . When you hear some preach . . . test the doctrines by the Scripture, as did the Bereans (Acts 17:11), and choose that which is best, soundest, and most true . . . There shall always be errors and heresies to test us, [and] we should also test them.[48]

Prophesying here signifies preaching, as it does in Romans 12:6 . . . The prophets are called "men of God" . . . If we should make much of prophets, how much should we make of prophesying? If we should love our instructors, how much should we love instruction? Simeon, staying in the temple, met with Christ. So many, hearing the word, have met with knowledge, with comfort, with peace, with salvation. But without the word never any was converted to God.[49]

Once Baal's prophets were punished, but now Christ's prophets are punished . . . If we be prophets, where is our reverence? When the preachers and teachers Christ sends to his Church are abused and persecuted . . . then he will remove their light and his gospel to others.[50]

The people's neglect of the prophets has made the prophets neglect prophesying . . . the drone never studies to preach. The second thing that makes prophets and prophesying despised is the lewdness and negligence of them that are able to do well in their ministry, yet do the contrary . . . by their slubbering of the Word, for lack of study and meditation . . . So the people stay at home, and say they know as much as the preacher can teach them.[51]

As every sound is not music, so every sermon is not preaching . . . As among rulers there be bad rulers, so among prophets there be false prophets . . . Try the spirits [by] the Word of God, the touchstone of everything . . . Believe nothing, but what it teaches, love nothing but what it prescribes, hate nothing but what it forbids, do nothing but what it commands.[52]

The Benefit of Contentation
I Timothy 6:6

I sought for a text which speaks against covetousness, which I may call the Londoner's sin . . . God has given you more than others, which should turn covetousness into thankfulness. Yet as the ivy grows with the oak, so covetousness has grown with riches . . . who within these walls thinks he has enough, though there be so many that have too much?

This is the devil who bewitches you, to think that you have not enough when you have more than you need . . . Paul craves your covetousness, that he might bury it . . . You have found little joy in money, you shall find great joy in the Holy Ghost. You have found little peace in the world, you shall find great peace in conscience. He that will have contentment must leave his covetousness in pawn for it (I Tim. 6:6).[53]

What has brought usury, simony, bribery, cruelty, subtilty, envy, strife, and deceit to this city . . . and made every shop a market of oaths, lies, and frauds, but the superfluous love of money? [Here] is the root of all evil . . . the spawn of all sin.[54]

It is against the name and nature of covetousness to be content, as it is against the name and nature of contentation to be covetous . . . No covetous man is God's servant, but God's enemy (Matt. 6:24; I John 2:15).[55]

God does not command men to be godly only because it makes for his glory, but because godliness is profitable to us . . . The godly shall do well in heaven and here, too . . . The gain of godliness is wealth, and peace, and joy, and love of God, and the remission of sins, and everlasting life . . . Godliness brings contentation.[56]

EIGHT

❧ JOHN BUNYAN ❧

1 6 2 8 — 8 8

"Bunyan was a man of many talents, including an ability to render the or-dinary life of his times in a pungently realistic fashion . . . his gift for ex-ploiting the dramatic potential of biblical metaphors in such a way as to give shape and meaning to the spiritual life of the people to whom he wrote." [1]

In The Pilgrim's Progress (1678), *Bunyan portrays Vanity Fair, Doubting Castle, River of Death, Water of Life, Slough of Despond, De-lectable Mountains, and more. Influenced by Luther's commentary on Galatians, he produced an autobiographical work entitled* Grace Abounding to the Chief of Sinners (1666). *Bunyan warned people through* The Life and Death of Mr. Badman (1680). *He described* The Holy War (1682), *also known as* The Holy War Made by Shad-dai upon Diabolus, *and held out hope to the worst of transgressors in* The Jerusalem Sinner Saved (1688).

Bunyan began preaching in 1655 but spent twelve years in prison for his nonconformist stand. Confined, he read Foxe's Book of Martyrs, Holy Scriptures, *and a biblical concordance. While in jail he began to write* The Pilgrim's Progress. *The career of this valiant member of the church militant definitely demonstrates the truth that "the word of God is not bound" (II Tim. 2:9).*

The Jerusalem Sinner Saved

One reason which moved me to write and print this little book was, because there are many excellent, heart-affecting discourses in the world that tend to convert the sinner, yet I had a desire to try this simple method of mine; wherefore I make bold thus to invite and encourage the worst to come to Christ for life . . . I have been vile myself but have obtained mercy.[2]

After he rose from the dead, Christ gave a commission to preach the gospel to all nations . . . "beginning at Jerusalem" (Luke 24:47). As to her descent [Jerusalem] was from Abraham . . . a people God singled out from the rest of the nations to set his love upon them . . . She was the place of God's worship . . . but now decayed, degenerated, and apostatized . . . greatly backslidden, and become the place where truth and true religion were much defaced.[3]

In a word, Jerusalem was now become the shambles, the very slaughter-shop for saints . . . wherein the prophets, Christ, and his people were most horribly persecuted and murdered. . . . This is the city and these are the people; this is their character and these are their sins.

I will now show you what it was to preach the gospel to them: [to announce] repentance and remission of sins in Christ's name . . . to bid them repent and believe the gospel (Luke 24:47; Mark 1:15).

Christ would have Jerusalem have the first offer of the gospel. Not because they had any more right than any of the nations of the world, [but to manifest] his mere grace . . . compassion . . . and mercy [to those] in the most deplorable condition of any people under the heavens.[4]

These therefore, must have the cream of the Gospel . . . The Lord Jesus takes more care, as appears by three parables, for the lost sheep, the lost groat, and the prodigal son, than for the other sheep, the other pence, or for the son that said he had never transgressed (Luke 15) . . . The mind of Christ was set on the salvation of the biggest sinners in his lifetime.

The apostles, after the ascension of Christ, preached to the very worst of these Jerusalem sinners, even to those that were the murderers of Jesus Christ (Acts 2:23). Peter said that if they were sorry for what they had done, and would be baptized for the remission of their sins in his name, they should receive the gift of the Holy Ghost (Acts 2:37, 38).[5]

How willing was Peter, and the Lord Jesus, by his ministry to catch these murderers with the word of the gospel, that they might be made monuments of the grace of God! How unwilling, I say, was he that any of these should escape the hand of mercy!

Is not this amazing grace? Christ will not be put off: these are the sinners that are sinners indeed . . . sinners of the biggest sort.

Men are shorter-winded, soon moved to take vengeance . . . But God is full of grace, full of patience, ready to forgive, as one that delights in mercy . . . Oh the greatness of the grace of Christ, that he should be thus in love with the souls of Jerusalem sinners![6]

The first Church, the Jerusalem Church, was a church made up of Jerusalem sinners. These great sinners were here the most shining monuments to the exceeding grace of God . . . when his ministers first began to preach there he joined his power to the word, to the converting of thousands of his betrayers and murderers, and also many of the ringleading priests, to the faith.

Christ would have mercy offered in the first place to the biggest sinners, to the Jerusalem sinners. Why? Because the biggest sinners have most need of it. He that has the most need should be helped first. "Begin at Jerusalem."[7]

Men that are at the point to die have more need of the physician than they that are but now and then troubled with a heart-fainting qualm (Mark 2:15–17). The publicans and sinners were in the mouth of death . . . therefore the Lord Jesus receives them first, offers them mercy first.[8]

This man has most need, he is furthest from God, nearest to hell, and so one that has the most need . . . of mercy.

Mercy arises from compassion . . . from a feeling of the condition of those in misery (Isa. 63:9; James 5:11) . . . Mercy seems to be out of its proper channel when it deals with self-righteous men; but it runs with a full stream when it extends itself to the biggest sinner.[9]

Christ Jesus would have mercy offered in the first place to the biggest sinner, because when they receive it, it rebounds most to the fame of his name (Jer. 23:8, 9). He saved Lot from the guilt and damnation that he had procured to himself by his incest. He saved David from the vengeance that belonged to him for committing adultery and murder. Also Solomon, Manasseh, Peter, Magdalen, and many others . . . here are their sins and their salvations, recorded together, that you may read and know what a Saviour he is, and do him honour in the world . . . He shows sinners what he can do, to the praise and glory of his grace.[10]

When Christ was crucified and hanged up between the earth and the heavens, there were two thieves crucified with him. Behold, he lays hold of one of them, and will have him away with him to glory. Was not this a strange act and a display of extraordinary grace?

Christ would have mercy offered in the first place to the biggest sinners because, by their forgiveness and salvation, others hearing of it will be encouraged all the more to come to him for life. For the physician, by curing the most desperate at the first, not only gets himself a name but begets encouragement in the minds of other diseased folk to come to him for help (Matt. 24:24, 25). As Christ did with outward cures, so he does in the proffers of his grace . . . to the biggest sinners, that others may take heart to come to him and be saved.[11]

"God, who is rich in mercy . . . loved us even when we were dead in our sins [and] quickened us together with Christ." Why did he do all this? "That in the ages to come he might show the exceeding riches of his grace, in his kindness towards us in Christ Jesus" (Eph. 2:4–7). So he allures others and their children to come to him and partake of the same grace through Christ Jesus.

As the Jerusalem sinners were of the highest sort among the Jews, so these Ephesian sinners were of the highest sort among the Gentiles (Eph. 2:1–3; 2:11, 12) . . . When God saves one great sinner, it is to encourage another great sinner to come to him for mercy.[12]

He saved the thief, to encourage thieves to come to him for mercy . . . He saved Saul, to encourage Sauls to come to him for mercy (I Tim. 1:16). In saving us, Christ has given to the world a pattern of his grace, that they might see and believe, and come and be saved—that they that are born thereafter might believe on Jesus Christ to life everlasting. [So Paul testifies in I Tim.1:14, 15, and David in Ps. 51:7–13].

The heart of man, though set in sin, will, when it once comes to a persuasion that God is willing to have mercy upon us, incline to come to Jesus Christ for life . . . Mercy is the antidote against sin . . . it will make the unwilling willing to come to Jesus Christ for life.[13]

Jesus Christ would have mercy offered in the first place to the biggest sinners because . . . if they receive it—that is the way to weaken the kingdom of Satan . . . The biggest sinners are Satan's colonels, captains, leaders [in the war] against the Son of God. Let these first be conquered, and his kingdom will be weak.

Christ came to destroy the works of the devil, and to destroy by converting grace as well as by redeeming blood . . . The way, the most direct way . . . is to deal with such sinners by the word of his gospel and by the merits of his passion . . . I speak by experience: I was one of these.[14]

Manasseh the king was a ringleading sinner, the great idolater, and chief of devilism. The whole land flowed with wickedness, "for he made them to sin" and to do worse than the heathen that dwelt round about them. But when God converted him, the whole land was reformed. Down went the groves, the idols, and altars of Baal, and up went true religion in much of the power and purity of it . . . The king reformed by [royal] power, and by example, too (II Chron. 33; II Kings 17:41).

When God takes hold of the hearts of the most notorious, this would make hell to sigh, to the great suppression of sin, the glory of Christ, and the joy of the angels of God.[15]

There are two things that great sinners are acquainted with when they come to divulge them to the saints: the conflicts that they usually have with the devil at their parting with him, and their knowledge of his secrets in his workings.[16]

Paul must go to the Gentiles, because Paul was the most outrageous of all the apostles in the time of his unregeneracy; and Peter must be he that after his horrible fall was thought fittest—when recovered again—to comfort and strengthen his brothers (Luke 22:31).

Christ would have mercy offered in the first place to the biggest sinners in that, when converted, they are apt to love him most (Luke 7:47) . . . He that has most sin, if forgiven, is partaker of the greatest love, of the greatest forgiveness.[17]

Paul laboured more than all—a labour of love—because he had been by sin more vile against Christ than they all (Gal. 1:3; 1 Cor. 15:9; Acts 26:11). What motivated him? The love of Christ (II Cor. 5:14). Paul was affected and carried away with the love and grace of God.[18]

When grace and the great sinner meet, and grace shall subdue that great sinner to itself, and shall operate after its kind in the soul of that great sinner, then we have a shining Christian . . . The Thessalonians were idolaters before the word of God came to them. But when they had received it, they became examples to all that did believe in Macedonia and Achaia (I Thess. 1:6–10).[19]

When the debauched ones that are to be saved shall be brought in, when these that look more like devils than men shall be converted to Christ, [and I believe several of them will], then will Christ be exalted, grace adored, the word prized, Zion's paths better trodden, and men in the pursuit of their own salvation to the amazement of them that are left behind.[20]

God's word has two edges . . . if it does you no good it will do you hurt. It is the savour of life to those that receive it, but of death unto death to them that refuse it (II Cor. 2:15, 16).[21]

No man shows himself willing to be saved that repents not of his deeds. For he that goes on still in his trespasses declares that he is resolved to pursue his own damnation.[22]

Learn to judge of the sufficiency of the merits of Christ . . . the unsearchable riches of Christ. Consider what offers he makes—after his resurrection—of his grace to sinners . . . There is sufficiency in his blood to save the biggest sinners (Acts 13:38, 39) . . . Remission of sins is through faith in his blood (Eph. 1:7) . . . The biggest of sinners cannot be saved but by the abundance of grace.

"It is a fearful thing to fall into the hands of the living God" (Heb. 10:31). He will grip hard, his fist is stronger than a lion's paw. Take heed of him. He will be angry if you despise his Son. And will you stand guilty in your trespasses when he offers you his grace and favour?[23]

The despair of devils, the despair of the damned, and the despair that a man has of attaining [eternal] life because of his own deficiency, are all reasonable. Why shouldn't devils and damned souls despair? Why shouldn't a man despair of getting to heaven by his own abilities?

Christ is able to save to the uttermost them that come to God through him. If he were not willing to save, he would not have commanded that mercy . . . should be offered to the biggest sinners. Unreasonable is the despair of those who would be saved, but are too strongly borne down with the burden of their sins . . . Come! (John 6:37; Isa. 55:1) . . . They that flee for refuge to the hope set before them have this promise and oath for their salvation (Heb. 6:17, 18).[24]

Despair undervalues the promise, undervalues the invitation, undervalues the proffer of grace. Despair undervalues the ability of God the Father and the redeeming blood of Christ his Son. Oh unreasonable despair!

As long as my eyes can find a promise in the Bible, as long as there is the least mention of grace, as long as there is a moment left me of breath or life in this world, so long will I wait or look for mercy, so long will I fight against unbelief and despair. This is the way to honour God and Christ. This is the way to set the crown on the promise . . . Never despair so long as our text is alive, because it announces and offers mercy through Christ.[25]

Only faith knows how to deal with mercy. Don't displace faith with presumption [wild faith]. Presumption puts itself in the place of faith when it tampers with the promise of life while the soul is a stranger to repentance. You have in the text, (Luke 24:47), to prevent doing thus, both repentance and remission of sins to be offered to Jerusalem; not remission without repentance, for all that repent not shall perish.

Men presume when they are resolved to abide in their sins, and yet expect to be saved by God's grace through Christ . . . It cannot be that God should be wheedled out of his mercy, or prevailed upon by lips of dissimulation. He knows them that trust in him and that sincerely come to him by Christ for mercy.[26]

Faith is the eye, the mouth, the hand . . . Faith is to see, to receive, to work or to eat. A Christian should be receiving, seeing, working, or feeding all day long. Let it rain, let it blow, let it thunder, let it lighten, a Christian must still believe.[27]

Let ministers follow the steps of their blessed Lord, who by word and deed showed his love to the salvation of the world in such a way as declared him to prefer their salvation before his own private concern.

Love your Saviour. Show one to another that you love him, not only by a seeming love of affection, but with the love of duty. Practical love is best. Many love Christ with nothing but the lick of the tongue. Alas!

The devil . . . knows that a loose professor in the Church does more mischief to religion than ten can do to it that are in the world.[28]

Like a king who of grace sends out to his rebellious people an offer of pardon if they accept it by such a day, yet beheads or hangs those that come not in for mercy until the expiry time be past, so Christ Jesus has set the sinner a day—a day of salvation—an acceptable time, but he who will not come and goes on in rebellion beyond that time, is liable to come off with the loss of his soul.

To slight grace, to despise mercy, and to stop the ear when God speaks . . . so much to our profit is a great provocation. He offers, he calls, he woos, he invites, he prays, he beseeches us, in this his day of grace. He has provided us with the means of reconciliation himself. This despising must needs be provoking.[29]

If God had said he will forgive one sin, it would have been unde-
served grace. But when he says he will pardon all but one, this is grace
of the highest order. Nor is that one unpardonable [sin] otherwise but
because the Saviour that should save them is rejected and put away.

We read of Jacob's ladder. Christ is Jacob's ladder that reaches
up to heaven, and he that refuses to go by this ladder will not,
though using other means, get up so high. There is none other
name given under heaven among men whereby we must be saved.
There is also none other sacrifice for sin than his. He also, and he
alone, is the Mediator that reconciles men to God. And sinner, if
you would be saved by him, his benefits are yours . . . even though
you are a great and Jerusalem transgressor.[30]

A Confession of Faith

Faith and holiness are my professed principles, with an endeavour—as far as lies in me—to be at peace with all men.

I believe that there is but one only true God: the Father, the
Word, and the Holy Ghost . . . I believe that there shall be a resurrection of the dead, both of the just and unjust . . . they that have
done good, to the resurrection of life, and they that have done evil,
to the resurrection of damnation (John 5:28, 29).

I believe . . . that none can be saved without the means of a
Redeemer . . . I believe that Jesus Christ our Lord is himself the Re-
deemer . . . I believe that he is both God and man, the Christ of the
Living God (Luke 2:10–14).

I believe that the righteousness and redemption by which believers stand just before God—saved from the curse of the law—is
the righteousness and redemption . . . of Jesus, the God-man (II
Cor. 5:19, 21).[31]

I believe that for the completing of this [saving] work he was
always sinless, did always the things that pleased God's justice . . . I
believe that the righteousness that saves the sinner from the wrath
to come is properly and personally Christ's, and ours in virtue of our
union with him, God by grace imputing it to us (Phil. 3:9).

I believe that God, as the reward of Christ's undertaking for us, has exalted him to his own right hand as our Mediator, given him a name above every name, and made him Lord of all, judge of the living and the dead (Phil. 2:5–11) . . . I believe that, being at the right hand of God in heaven, he does there effectually exercize all the offices of his excellent priesthood and mediatorship (Heb. 4:4–16; Rom. 8:33, 34).

I believe that . . . he shall come again in glory, and sit in judgment upon all (Matt. 25:31–46; Acts 1:9–11; I Thess. 4:13–18).[32]

I believe, we being sinful creatures in ourselves, that no good thing done by us can procure of God the imputation of the righteousness of Christ. That imputation is an act of grace, a free gift without our deserving (Rom. 3:23–26) . . . I believe that offer of this righteousness, as tendered in the gospel, is to be received by faith (Acts 13:38, 39; Rom. 5:1) . . . Faith receives, accepts, embraces, and trusts God's offer (John 1:12; I Tim. 1:15) . . . I believe that such faith is found only in those in whom the Spirit of God, by mighty power, does work it. All others, being fearful and incredulous, dare not venture their souls and eternity upon it.

I believe that this faith is effectually wrought in none but those which, before the world, were ordained unto eternal life (Acts 13:48; I Thess. 1:1–10).[33]

I believe that election is free and permanent, being founded in grace and the unchangeable will of God. I believe that we are predestinated to be conformed to the image of his Son (Rom. 8:29, 30).

I believe that without Christ Jesus there is neither election, grace, nor salvation (Eph. 1:3–14) . . . I believe that no man can know his election but by his calling . . . Election does not foretell or prevent the means which are appointed of God to bring us to Christ, to grace, and to glory (II Pet. 1:8–11).

I believe that in effectual calling the Holy Ghost must accompany the work of the gospel, and that with mighty power . . . Calling is the fruit of electing love (I Thess. 1:4–10) . . . an effectual awakening about the evil of sin, and especially of unbelief . . . and great awakenings about the world to come and the glory of unseen things.[34]

I believe that in effectual calling there is also a sanctifying virtue; and hence we are said to be called with an holy calling, with an heavenly calling, called to glory and virtue (I Pet. 2:9, 10) . . . I believe that effectual calling produces faith (Rom. 10:14–17) . . . hope . . . and repentance.

Repentance is a turning of the heart to God in Christ . . . a turning from sin, and the devil, and darkness, to the goodness, and grace, and holiness that is in him . . . Godly repentance does not only affect the soul with the loathsome nature of sin that is past, but fills the heart with godly hatred for sins that yet may come.[35]

I believe that effectual calling . . . also produces love. That is why Paul, when he had put the Church in remembrance that they were called of God, adds that concerning brotherly love they had no need that he should write to them . . . If God be so kind to us to forgive us our sins, save our souls, and give us the kingdom of heaven, let these be motives beyond all other, to provoke us to love again. If we that are thus beloved of God are made members of one body, all partakers of his grace, all clothed with his glorious righteousness, and are appointed to be the children of God of the next world, should we not love one another?[36]

I believe and confess that all the Holy Scriptures are the words of God. "All Scripture is given by inspiration of God" (II Tim. 3:16). "The prophecy of the Scriptures came not in old time by the will of man, but holy men of God spake as they were moved by the Holy Ghost" (II Pet. 1:21).

I believe that the Holy Scriptures, of themselves, without the addition of human inventions, are able to make the man of God perfect in all things, and thoroughly to furnish him unto all good works. They are able to make you wise unto salvation, through faith in Christ Jesus, and to instruct you in all other things that either respect the worship of God or your lifestyle before all men.

I believe that the great end why God committed the Scriptures to writing was, that we might be instructed [directed] to
Christ, taught how to believe, encouraged to patience and hope for
the grace that is to be brought to us at the revelation of Jesus Christ;
also that we might understand what sin is, and how to avoid its
commission (Ps. 119:105).

I believe that they [the Scriptures] cannot be broken, but will
certainly be fulfilled in all the prophecies, threatenings, and
promises, either to the salvation or damnation of men.

I believe Jesus Christ, by the word of the Scriptures, will judge
all men at the day of doom (II Cor. 5:10; Rev. 20:11–15).

I believe that this God made the world and all things that are
therein . . . When the Most High divided to the nations their inheritance, when he separated the sons of Adam, he set the bounds
of the people according to the number of the children of Israel.

I believe that magistracy [civil government] is God's ordinance, which he has appointed for the government of the whole
world, and that it is a judgment of God to be without those ministers which he has ordained to put wickedness to shame (Rom.
13:1–7; I Pet. 2:13–17) . . . Many are the mercies we receive by a
well-qualified magistrate; and if any shall at any time be otherwise
inclined, let us show our Christianity in a patient suffering for well-
doing what it shall please God to inflict by them.[37]

NINE

WILLIAM GURNALL

1617–79

William Gurnall was educated at Cambridge, appointed to Lavenham in 1644, and made "rector for life" by Parliament. At the time of the Restoration, he signed the Act of Uniformity and was attacked by some nonconforming clergy as one numbered among "covenant-renouncers and desperate apostates." He nevertheless continued in pastoral ministry as one committed to the Reformed faith. His book on Ephesians 6:10–12, "The Christian in Complete Armour: A Treatise of the Saint's War against the Devil" *is a classic on spiritual conflict and victory.*

Our generation has seen the ruinous power of the demonic in the brutalitarian regimes that have resulted in systematic racism, ethnic cleansing, genocide, and the holocaust. Yet it does not take the factor of moral evil seriously, and thus compounds the problem. The Puritans did not have to be convinced about the reality of evil, or of the Evil One. Recall Bunyan's Holy War *and William Gouge's treatise on* The Whole Armour of God, *as well as Gurnall on* The Christian in Complete Armour, *first published in three volumes, between 1655 and 1662.*

The Christian in Complete Armour

The subject of the treatise is solemn: *A War Between the Saint and Satan* . . . The stage whereon this war is fought, is every man's own soul. Here is no neuter in this war. The whole world is engaged in the quarrel, either for God and against Satan, or for Satan and against God . . .[1]

The drum beats in the gospel for volunteers . . . Let none take your crown from you . . . Be thankful for every victory you get . . . He is the right soldier that is not discouraged by those that run from, or that are slain in the battle, but still press on to victory . . . March on, not in the confidence of your armour, but in the power of his might, who has promised shortly to subdue Satan under your feet.[2]

With undaunted courage march on, and be strong in the Lord, on whose performance lies the stress of the battle, and not on your skill or strength . . . It requires more prowess and greatness of spirit to obey God faithfully, than to command an army of men; to be a Christian than a captain . . .

The Christian is to proclaim and prosecute an irreconcilable war against . . . those sins that have lain nearest his heart . . . [3]

The Christian must stand fixed to his principles [showing] his holy constancy in the truth . . . This persevering is a hard word! This taking up the cross daily, this praying always, this watching night and day . . . waiting on God, and walking with God.[4]

The sweet bait of religion has drawn many to nibble at it, who are offended with the hard service to which it calls. It requires another spirit than the world can give or receive to follow Christ fully . . . Say not that you have royal blood running in your veins and are begotten of God, except you can prove your pedigree by this heroic spirit, to dare to be holy in spite of men and devils . . .

How uncomely a sight it is to see a bold sinner and a fearful saint, one resolved to be wicked, and a Christian wavering in his holy course . . . Take heart therefore, you saints, and be strong; your cause is good . . . God has appointed his Son . . . the Captain of our salvation.[5]

The Christian's strength lies in the Lord, not in himself . . . He is the strength of all his saints in their war against sin and Satan.[6]

Does the Christian's strength lie in God, not in himself? This may forever keep the Christian humble . . . Walk humbly, therefore, before your God.[7]

To be strong in the power of the Lord's might implies two acts of faith. First, a settled firm persuasion that the Lord is almighty in power . . . Second, to believe that this almighty power of God is engaged for its defense, so as to bear up in the midst of all trials and temptations undauntingly, leaning on the arm of God Almighty . . . The dear love he bears his saints engages his power. He that has God's heart cannot lack his arm.[8]

It is not a man's morality and philosophical nature that will repel a temptation sent with a full charge from Satan's cannon . . . The graces of Christ—these are armour . . . To be without Christ is to be without armour . . . unfit to fight Christ's battles against sin and Satan . . . [9]

The Christian must be in complete armour, in regard to the several pieces and weapons that make up the whole armour of God. Indeed there is a concatenation of graces—they hang together like links in a chain, stones in an arch, members in the body . . . The Christian's armour is made to be worn . . . till we have done our warfare and finished our course.[10]

The saint's enemy is the devil . . . a very subtle enemy. The Christian is endangered most by his policy and craft . . . His first main design is to draw into sin. The second main design is to accuse, vex, and trouble the saint for sin . . . molesting the saint's peace and disquieting the saint's spirit . . . Satan is first a tempter, and then a troubler.[11]

If you would be guarded from him as a troubler, take heed of him as a seducer . . . Study that grand gospel truth of a soul's justification before God . . . Get into this tower of the gospel covenant, and roll this truth on the head of Satan. Be careful to keep your old receipts which you received from God for the pardon of your sins.[12]

Satan, with all his wits and wiles, shall never vanquish a soul armed with true grace.[13]

The Christian's state in this life is one of combat . . . He needs his sword as much as his trowel . . . The Christian is assailed on every side by his enemy. How can it be otherwise, when the seeds of war are laid deep in the natures of both, and can never be rooted up till the devil cease to be a devil, sin to be sin, and saint to be a saint? . . . Sin will lust against grace, and grace draw upon sin, whenever they meet.[14]

How this [conflict] should make the Christian long to be gone home, where there is none of this stir and scuffle . . . Every hour seems not a day, and every day a year, till death sounds your joyful retreat, and calls you off the field . . . to come to court, where not swords but palms are seen in the saint's hands; not drums but harps; not groans of bleeding soldiers and wounded consciences, but sweet and ravishing music is heard of triumphant victors carolling the praises of God and the Lamb, through whom they have overcome . . . Comfort yourselves with these things. There is a place of rest remaining for the people of God.[15]

Heaven is not won with good words and a fair profession . . . The doing Christian is the man that shall stand, when the empty boaster of his faith shall fall. The great talkers of religion are oft the least doers. His religion is in vain whose profession brings not letters testimonial of a holy life. Sacrifice without obedience is sacrilege.[16]

He that will be Christ's soldier must persevere to the end of his life in this war against Satan . . . There is no such a thing [in] Christianity as an honourable retreat; not such a word in all Christ's military discipline, as fall back and lay down your arms . . . You must stand to your arms till called off by death.[17]

To stand at the end of this war will abundantly recompense all our hazard and hardship involved in the war against sin and Satan . . . To stand is to [be] justified and acquitted at the great day of judgment . . . Shall not the joy of heaven which is set before the Christian, into which he shall assuredly enter, make him run his race, endure a short scuffle of temptation and affliction? These are not worthy to be compared with the glory which shall be revealed . . . [18]

Stand manfully . . . make good your ground against the enemy, by a valiant receiving of his charge and repelling his force . . . Satan in his temptations is stoutly to be resisted.[19]

Stand firm with the belt of truth buckled around your waist . . . Some by truth mean truth of doctrine; others will have it truth of heart, sincerity . . . Both are required to make the belt complete . . . sincerity to propound a right end, and knowledge of the word of truth to direct us in the right way to that end . . . [20]

If the understanding be clear in its apprehension of truth, and the will sincere, vigorous, and fixed in its purposes for that which is holy and good, then he is a strong Christian . . . Satan comes as a serpent in the persons of false teachers, [or] as a lion in the persons of bloody persecutors . . . To defend us against this, we need to have truth girt about us, so that with a holy resolution we may maintain our profession in the face of death and danger.[21]

Live by your own faith, not another's. Labour to see truth with your own eyes . . . Let not authority from man, but evidence from the word, conclude your judgment . . . There is surely a mean between defying men and deifying them. It is the admiring of persons that forms the traitor to truth, and makes many cry "Hosanna" to error, and "Crucify" to truth . . . Despise none, adore none.[22]

Many that could never be beaten from the truth by dint of argument, have been forced from it by fire of persecution . . . It is the saint's duty . . . to maintain a steadfast profession of the truth . . . He that staggers is next door to apostasy.[23]

Sincerity has a preserving strength to keep the soul from the defilements of sin. When temptation comes . . . a false heart is put to the run, it cannot possibly stand . . . Sincerity keeps the soul from the power of temptation . . . On the contrary, hypocrisy weakens and unsettles the heart.[24]

Labour for sincerity. Without it we can neither stand against, nor rise when we fall into temptation. Whatever you beg of God, forget not a sincere heart . . . Crowns and diadems are not to be compared with it . . . Nothing makes you more like God in the simplicity and purity of his nature, than sincerity.[25]

All Christ's soldiers should have on the breastplate of righteousness . . . Scripture speaks of a . . . perfect personal and perpetual obedience . . . Not the holiest saint that ever lived can stand righteous before the bar [of God's justice] . . . The second righteousness which the Scripture speaks of is an *evangelical* righteousness—a righteousness imputed or imparted. The *imputed* righteousness is that which is wrought by Christ *for* the believer; the *imparted,* that which is wrought by Christ *in* the believer [or] the righteousness of our justification [and] the righteousness of our sanctification.[26]

The righteousness wrought by Christ in the believer . . . is a supernatural principle of a new life implanted in the heart of every child of God by the powerful operation of the Holy Spirit whereby they endeavour to approve themselves to God and man, in performing what the word of God requires to be performed to both . . . Who, but the Spirit of God, can make a creature like God, by making him a partaker of the divine nature?[27]

A truly sanctified heart dares not skip or blot one word God has written, but desires to be a faithful executor to perform the whole will of God.[28]

Why are righteousness and holiness compared to the breastplate?
The breastplate preserves the principal part of the body . . . where a shot or stab is more deadly than in other parts that are remote from the fountain of life . . . Thus righteousness and holiness preserve the principal part of a Christian . . . his soul and conscience.

The breastplate, by defending this principal part, emboldens the soldier, and makes him fearless of danger . . . Righteousness, by defending the conscience, fills the creature with courage in the face of death and danger, whereas guilt—which is the nakedness of the soul—puts the stoutest sinner into a shaking fit of fear.[29]

Keep on the breastplate of righteousness. Exhibit the power of a holy and righteous life. First, in regard to God, whose great design is to have his people "a holy people." Second, with reference to Satan, whose design is as much against the saints' holiness as God is for it. Third, with respect to holiness itself, the incomparable excellency of which commands us to pursue it.

He who means to be a Christian indeed must endeavour to maintain the power of holiness and righteousness in his life and conversation . . . He is a holy righteous man that has a work of grace and holiness in his heart.[30]

Without holiness no man shall see the Lord. Heaven is a city where righteousness dwells . . . It is holiness that fits us for communion with God in this life . . . The Spirit of God gives the lie to that man who says he has any acquaintance with God, while he keeps his acquaintance with any unrighteousness . . . Communion is founded on union, and union upon likeness . . . An unholy heart has no dealings with God; he takes no notice of God . . . [31]

Holiness is necessary to the true peace and repose of the soul . . . Holiness has a mighty influence upon others: it stops the mouths of the ungodly . . . and is a means to open their very hearts to the embracing of Christ and his grace. [32]

The third piece of armour in the Christian's panoply is a spiritual shoe. His feet are shod with the preparation of the gospel of peace.

What is meant by the gospel? The good news, the joyful message of Christ and salvation by him to poor sinners . . . gospel grace, pardoning mercy. No good news can come before it . . . no ill news can come after the glad tidings of the gospel . . . This is the great se-

cret which God whispers by his Spirit, in the ears of those only
whom he embraces with special distinguishing love.[33]

Christian, as you sit at feast of the gospel, think of those poor
souls . . . who starve to death for want of that bread with which you
are fed to eternal life.[34]

What peace is attributed to the gospel?
True peace is the blessing of the gospel and only of the gospel.
First, peace with God, which we may call peace of reconciliation.
Second, peace with ourselves, or peace of conscience. Third, peace
with one another, or peace of love and unity. Fourth, peace with
other creatures, even the most hurtful, which may be called a peace
of indemnity and service.

When man fell out with God, he fell out with himself, and all
the world besides; and he can never come to peace with these, till
his peace be made with God.[35]

The gospel presents us with the articles of peace which God
graciously offers to treat and conclude an inviolable peace upon,
with rebellious man . . . The gospel is but God's heart in print . . .

The guilty creature is surrounded on every side as with a del-
uge of wrath—no hope nor help to be heard of—till the gospel, like
the dove, brings the olive branch of peace . . . The tide is turned,
and that flood of wrath which was poured on man for his sin is now
fallen into another channel, even upon Christ, who was "made a
curse for us." "Being justified by faith, we have peace with God
through our Lord Jesus Christ." We are entirely beholden to the
gospel for the discovery of this secret.[36]

The fourth piece in the Christian's panoply . . . is the shield of
faith. Justifying faith. A grace that makes him the devil's match
. . . not a naked assent to the truths of the gospel [but] an act of the
soul whereby it rests on Christ crucified for pardon and life, and
that upon the warrant of [God's] promise.

Faith is . . . a shield intended for the defense of the whole body
. . . Sometimes temptation is levelled at the head . . . against this
truth and that, to make the Christian call them into question . . .

blot out the deity of Christ, with other mysterious truths of the gospel . . . Now faith comes between the Christian and this arrow. It comes into the relief of the Christian's weak understanding.[37]

Is it *conscience* that the tempter assaults? It is not seldom that he is shooting his fiery darts of horror and terror at this mark. Faith receives the shock, and saves the creature . . . [38]

Is it the *will* that the temptation is laid to catch? Some commands of God cannot be obeyed without much self-denial, because they cross us in that which our own wills are carried forth very strongly to desire; so that we must deny our will before we can do the will of God . . . Now faith is the grace that renders the soul admirable service at such a crisis as this . . . By faith, Abraham obeyed . . . It was hard work for Moses . . . to enter upon his labours . . . Yet faith made him willing.[39]

The fifth piece in the Christian's panoply to cover his head in the day of battle: the helmet of salvation . . . Or, if we consult another text, the hope of salvation.[40]

Hope is a supernatural grace of God, whereby the believer, through Christ, expects and waits for all those good things of the promise, which at present he has not fully or partly received.

True hope is a jewel that none wears but Christ's bride . . . Hope's object is all that the promise holds forth . . . the hope of glory, the hope of eternal life, the hope of salvation . . . It brings the Christian and heaven together, as if he were there already.[41]

Why is hope compared to a helmet? The helmet defends the head . . . from dint of bullet and sword . . . This hope defends the soul . . . whereby no dangerous or deadly impression can by Satan or sin be made on it . . . As the helmet defends the soldier's head from wounding, so his heart also from swooning. It makes him bold and fearless in battle.

A man cannot drown so long as his head is above water. Now it is the proper function of hope to do this for the Christian in times of danger . . . Two things make the head hang down—fear and shame. Hope eases the Christian's heart of both . . . and so forbids him to give any sign of a desponding mind by a dejected countenance.[42]

The sixth and last piece in the Christian's panoply: the sword of the Spirit, which is the word of God . . . By the edge of this, his enemies fall and all his great exploits are done . . . As it defends the soldier, so it offends his enemy. By it he kills and mortifies his lusts within, and this makes his victory complete.[43]

The Holy Scriptures are the undoubted word of God . . . that one foundation on which our faith is built . . . the doctrine which God delivered to his church under the unerring guidance of the Spirit . . . from the very mind and heart of God.

An enlightened conscience and sanctified heart will be commanded by the overpowering evidence that shines forth in the Scriptures to fall down and cry: It is the voice of God.[44]

The Scripture . . . has a heart-searching power; whereby it ransacks and rifles the conscience of men. It exercizes a power on the conscience to convince and terrify it. It has a power to comfort and raise a dejected spirit. It has the power of conversion, which none but God can effect.[45]

When souls are converted, "the blind receive their sight" . . . "the lame walk" in that the affections are set at liberty and receive strength to run the ways of God with delight. Lepers are cleansed, in that filthy crusts are cured, and foul souls are sanctified . . . Such changes are the daily product of "the word."[46]

Satan, being a spirit, must be fought with spiritual arms. And such is the word, a spiritual sword, [whose] Author is the Holy Spirit . . . The Scriptures must be read, and can be understood, by that Spirit alone.

That written word is the sword by which the Spirit of God enables saints to overcome all their enemies . . . All the great conquests which Christ and his saints achieve in the world are got with this sword.[47]

Bless God for these three mercies in reference to the Scriptures: for their translation into the language of the people; for the ministry of the word; for the efficacy of the word on your heart.[48]

Furnish yourselves with the armour of God, and join prayer to all these graces for your defense against your spiritual enemies . . . Prayer is a necessary duty to be performed by the Christian . . . in all his undertakings, enjoyments, and temptations.[49]

Prayer is a channel of grace, for the conveying of blessings from God . . . a means of worship, whereby we are to do our homage to God and give him the glory of his deity . . . a humble appeal from our impotency to God's omnipotence.

In prayer we do not only beg mercy of God, but vow praise to God for the mercies we beg . . . [so that] we wear with thankfulness what we win by prayer.[50]

Now Satan's designs against prayer are of three kinds. First, if he can, he will keep you from prayer. Second, he will strive to interrupt you in prayer. Third, if that plot fails, he will labour to hinder the success and return of your prayer.[51]

To pray in faith is to ask of God, in the name of Christ, what he has promised, relying on his power and truth for performance . . . This reliance of the soul . . . fastens on God like the anchor's double hook. It takes hold on the power of God . . . and the faithfulness of God to perform the promise.[52]

TEN

❧ JOHN HOWE ❧

1 6 3 0 — 1 7 0 5

Son of a pastor who suffered exile for his nonconformist views, John Howe also endured ejection
from his parish in 1662. He had prepared for the
gospel ministry by studies at Cambridge and Oxford. About 1652, he served as pastor at Great
Torrington in Devonshire. There, lengthy worship
services were not infrequent, with a recess for
ministerial refreshment at the midway point, while
the congregation filled the break with singing.

Meeting Oliver Cromwell in London (1654), he was reluctantly
persuaded to become one of his chaplains. Howe showed a tolerant spirit
towards clerics of divergent convictions in a time of tension. When the
Act of Uniformity was passed, however, he refused to conform and
preached in private houses. Howe's preaching was without notes yet solid
in content. In an age of agitation, he showed an irenic disposition and
promoted Christian unity. His writings include Delighting in God
(1674), The Living Temple (1676, 1702), and The Redeemer's
Tears Over Lost Souls (1684).

The Living Temple

God is, and is conversable with men, or is such as is capable and apt
to receive worship from men, and impart blessedness to them. [But]
a cloud and darkness are now drawn over the world of mankind.

And though it be still very easily discernible that *God is*, it is yet more difficult to attain to so distinct apprehensions *what* he is, as are necessary to our conversing with him. Against this difficulty, he has afforded a gracious relief—that is, he has provided there should be a more express discovery of him extant among men, than can be collected by their observations upon this world. The case was such with man [now as great a stranger to God] as to require a written revelation of his nature and will. We have it in those Scriptures . . . the word of God.[1]

These holy writings were not intended . . . to inform us of God's existence, which they [pre]suppose, but to teach us our duty towards him, and what our expectations may be from him. They give us a true representation and discovery of his nature . . . and then, of the present state of things between him and us, that we might be directed how to apply ourselves to him suitably.[2]

Can there be any converse between God and men? How can it not be? How strange that there is not more! That he has not a temple in every human breast, replenished with his vital presence! That there are nothing but ruins and desolation to be found, where one would expect a fabric worthy of God, and an indwelling Deity![3]

Adore the grace that returns him to us, and inclined him to take that strange course . . . to repair his forlorn temple, and fill this desolate, forsaken world with the joyful sound of those glad tidings, "The tabernacle of God is with men."

Our discourse must here proceed by these steps, to show: 1. That mankind has universally revolted, and been in a state of apostasy from God; 2. That hereby the temple of God in man has been generally made waste and desolate; 3. That he has laid both the new foundation and the platform of his present temple in Immanuel, God with us, his own incarnate Son, who rebuilds, beautifies, furnishes, inhabits it, and orders all its concernments.

They that have read the sacred volume cannot be ignorant that all flesh have corrupted their way; that the great God, looking down from heaven . . . has only the unpleasing prospect before his eyes of a universal depravation and defection . . . This was not the first state of man, but he is degenerated into it from a former and better state . . . Even many who have never conversed with those sacred records have no less clearly discovered their sense of man's present evil state . . . How far he has swerved from what he was is easily conjecturable by comparing him with the measures which show what he should be . . . We neither are, nor do what we should!

Man is corrupted from his primitive integrity, and become a depraved and degenerate thing . . . By this degeneracy, the temple of the living God among men became waste and desolate, uninhabitable or unfit for his blessed presence . . . The divine image [is] now defaced and torn down . . . Instead of a temple, man is a cage of every unclean and hurtful thing . . . full of unrighteousness, fornication, wickedness, covetousness, maliciousness, envy, murder . . . How repugnant, in all respects, to the holy, pure, benign, merciful nature of God! How remote from the imitation of his Maker!

Thus is the true image of God torn down from his own temple, and become the temple of a false God, dedicated to that abominable idol, self.

It is no wonder that the blessed God absents himself and is become a stranger to this once beloved mansion . . . The stately ruins are visible to every eye and bear this doleful inscription: Here God once dwelt . . . The lamps are extinct, the altar overturned; the light and love are now vanished . . . the golden candlestick is displaced to make room for the throne of the prince of darkness . . . Look upon the fragments . . . the yet legible precepts that relate to practice . . . engraven by the finger of God, and how they now lie torn and scattered . . . The truth which is after godliness is not so much disbelieved, as hated, held in unrighteousness . . . The faded glory, the darkness, the disorder, the impurity, the decayed state . . . too plainly show the great inhabitant is gone.

When God left his temple, he did not consume it . . . Whatsoever was necessary [for its restoration] is designed and done at his own dear expense—his only begotten Son most freely consenting with him . . . sustaining the weight and burden of this great undertaking.[4]

The blessed God has laid the platform and the foundations of his temple, as it was to be restored and set up again among men, in and by that great Emmanuel, his own Son made flesh . . . an incarnate God among men, and a Man inhabited by all the fulness of God . . . a most perfect temple . . . "God with us."

Here [in Christ] were met together man that could die, and God that could overcome death; man that might suffer, and God that could give sufficient value to those sufferings; sufficient to atone the offended Majesty, and procure that life might be diffused . . . to all that should unite with him, whereby they might become living stones, joined to that living cornerstone—a spiritual temple, again capable of that divine presence which they had forfeited and whereof they were forsaken.

God was to have the first and leading part in reconciliations, as man has in disagreements.[5]

The sacrifice of him who was man was suitable to the offence of man; and of him who was God, was equal to the wrong done to God . . . The profanation of the former temple was expiated by the immolation of the new . . . Christ has redeemed us from the curse of the law (Gal. 3:13), being made a curse for us . . . Emmanuel was first made a personal temple, then a sacrifice.[6]

What sort of temple are we to be? Not of wood and stone . . . but temples by self-dedication, separating ourselves to that purpose . . . [So we] render back to God his own temple, most willingly, not merely from an apprehension of his right, but as overcome by his love.[7]

Here [in Christ] is the fairest representation that ever this world had or that could be had, of this most delectable object. The Divine holiness incarnate did never shine so bright. And we may easily apprehend the great advantage of having so lively and perfect a model set before us of what we are to design and aim at. Rules and precepts could never have afforded so full a description or have furnished us with so perfect an idea.

Look steadily to Jesus, "with open face" behold the glory of the Lord, and be "changed from glory to glory, as by the Spirit of the Lord" (II Cor. 3:18).

Truth is the means of holiness (John 17:17) . . . We have this practical truth not only exhibited in aphorisms and maxims in the Word, but we have it exemplified in the life of Christ. And when the great renovating work is to be done, the old man to be put off, the new man to be put on, the spirit of our mind to be renewed, our business is to learn Christ and the truth as it is in Jesus (Eph. 4:20–24).[8]

There could be no restoration of this temple of God . . . without the concurrence of these two things: the remission of sins, and the emission of the Holy Spirit. [Both come from] the rich sufficiency of Emmanuel.[9]

Without union with Christ, no man can have either his righteousness or his indwelling Spirit. Nor can they be separable . . . It is an unsupposable thing, that one should be God's temple enlivened and animated by his own Spirit, and yet be under remaining guilt and liable every moment to his consuming wrath. Or, that he could be any whit the better to have all his former guilt taken off and still be "dead in trespasses and sins."[10]

The communication of the Spirit was necessary to the restoring of this temple. The constitution of Emmanuel was necessary to the communication of the Spirit.

God's own judgment is the surest measure to direct ours . . . We are to reckon it always safe and modest to follow him, by an obsequious, ductile judgment of things apparent, and which he offers to our view, or appeals to us about them. To go before him by a preventive judgment of the secret things that belong to him, or pretend to give reasons, or an account of his matters where he gives none himself, argues rashness, arrogance, and self-confidence whereof we can give no account.[11]

It ought to be deeply considered, both as a truth of clearest evidence and great importance (though perhaps it may have escaped the thoughts of many) that the principal end of our Lord's undertaking and office was not the salvation of men but the glory of God. This is that whereupon his design did ultimately terminate . . . Otherwise he should make the creature his chief end (John 12:27, 28; Phil. 2:9–11).[12]

That admirable goodness of God, which shows itself in raising up temples in this vile world by the Spirit of Emmanuel, claims our subordinate cooperation as underbuilders in this structure (Phil. 2:12, 13).

The whole work of faith—that entire work necessary to be wrought upon the soul of man in order to his future felicity, and that by God's own power—is called the fulfilling or satisfying, the good pleasure of his goodness (II Thess. 1:11). Oh the plentitude of satisfaction which our blessed Lord takes in the fulfilling of the good pleasure of his goodness, when the methods are complied with, according whereto he puts forth his power for effecting such a work![13]

The Holy Spirit is given to this purpose of restoring the temple of God with men . . . under a two-fold notion: as a builder and an inhabitant.

Till this blessed Spirit be given, the temple of God is everywhere in ruin. Therefore, he cannot dwell till he build, and he builds that he may dwell (I Cor. 3:9, 16) . . . This temple, being a living thing, the very building and formation of it is . . . generating. And because it is to be again raised up out of a former ruinous state wherein it lay dead and buried in its own ruins, this new production is regeneration . . . This new birth must be by the Spirit (Eph. 2:19–22).[14]

The Spirit is given for Christ's sake . . . in his name . . . in consideration of his sufferings and death (John 14:26; Gal. 3:14).[15]

The Spirit is given for the restoring of God's temple with men, for the sake of Christ's death and sufferings, who was Emmanuel, and in his own person the *original temple* out of which each single temple was to arise . . . as well as he was the *exemplary temple* unto which they were all to be conformed.

The Spirit is given to implant what was necessary, root out what should be finally repugnant, either to their duty towards him or their felicity in him.[16]

When that first evangelical promise was collaterally and implicitly given (Gen. 3:15), wrapt up in the threatening to the serpent—that the woman's seed should break his head—it could mean no less than that he who should afterwards in the fulness of time become her seed and be born of a woman should redeem us from under the curse and turn it . . . upon himself. It was therefore also plain that no breath of holy, divine influence was ever to touch the spirit of man, had it not been for the Redeemer's interposition and undertaking.[17]

The Son of God, by consent with the Father, acts as a plenipotentiary and sovereign, quickening whom he will. The Spirit, by consent with him, breathes where it wills—as the wind—in order to the vital production of temples, or for regeneration.

For the purpose of inhabiting this temple, when by regeneration it is thus built and prepared, the Redeemer gives the Spirit . . . It is a thing full of wonder that he should be so far concerned in our affairs: to be incarnate for us, to be made a sacrifice for us, that he might have it in his power to give the Spirit, having become a curse for us, that he might be capable of conferring blessing upon us.[18]

The regenerate, as such, are sons both by receiving a new nature in their regeneration, and a new title in their adoption . . . Because they are sons, therefore, God sends the Spirit of his Son into their hearts (Gal. 4:6), and he is styled the Spirit of adoption (Rom. 8:14, 15.)

Receiving the Son . . . and believing in his name, they have authority or right to become the sons of God (John 1:12), being also regenerate, born not of flesh and blood—but of God. And thus, by faith receiving him, by faith they retain him, or have him abiding in them, as they abide in him. Their union is intimate and mutual (John 15:5).

What was lately a ruinous heap is become an animated temple, inhabited by the Divine presence. Where one person of the

Godhead is present, there the whole Trinity is present. Amazing thing!

The Old and New Testament evince the right which believers—they who are God's own people—have to the abiding indwelling presence of his Spirit as the inhabitant of that temple which they are now become. [All this is through] Emmanuel, the founder and restorer of this temple.[19]

It is the Mediator's part to bring the covenanting parties together. He is therefore said to be the Mediator of the new covenant (Heb. 12:24). He rendered it possible, by the merit of his blood, that the offended Majesty of heaven might—without injury to himself—consent; and that the Spirit might be given to procure our consent, which as Mediator or Emmanuel he gives. When he gives it in so copious an effusion as to be victorious, to conquer our aversion, and make us cease to be rebellious, then he enters to dwell (Ps. 68:18).

The known and usual summary of this covenant, on God's part, is "I will be their God." Now what can be meant . . . by his being their God, than giving them his indwelling Spirit? (II Cor. 6:16) . . . Why is his constant inhabiting presence to be with them? They will have no God if they have not with them and in them a divine, vital, inspiriting, inactuating presence to govern, quicken, support, and satisfy them, and fill them with an all-sufficient fulness. Else . . . they would be the temple of idol gods. It is therefore evident that this summary of God's part of his covenant—"I will be their God"—very principally intends his indwelling in them by his Spirit.

The [pledge] to be his people . . . signifies their faith, by which they take hold of his covenant, accept him to be their God, dedicate themselves to be his people, his very own possession, his mansion, his temple, wherein he may dwell. Now this self-resigning faith, taken in its just latitude, carries with it a two-fold reference to him as their sovereign Lord and their supreme good—whom, above all, they are to obey and enjoy. But can they obey him if he do not put his Spirit into them, to write his law on their hearts and cause them to walk in his statutes? (Ezek. 36:27). Or can they enjoy him, if they love him not as their supreme good?[20]

The grace of justification, pardon of sin, and adoption, are promised in the covenant, and upon faith, which is our taking hold of and entering into the covenant, our accepting God in Christ to be our God, and giving up ourselves to be his people . . . and repentance. For a sinner, one before in a state of apostasy from God, cannot take him to be his God, unless he exercize repentance towards God. His very act of taking him, in Christ, is turning to him, through Christ, from the sin by which he had departed and apostatized from him.[21]

Consider what punishment a sinner was, by the violated law of works and nature, liable to in this world or in the world to come. And what of this [punishment] is remitted in virtue of the Redeemer's sacrifice and covenant. He was liable to whatsoever miseries in this life God should please to inflict, to temporal death, and to a state of misery hereafter. [But] Christ has redeemed us from the curse of the law, being made a curse for us, that blessing might come upon us . . . that we might receive the promise of the Spirit (Gal. 3:13, 14).

"Repent, be baptized, for the remission of sins, and receive the Holy Ghost" (Acts 2:38). The great promise of the gospel covenant is that of the gift of the Holy Ghost. It does not promise you worldly wealth, or ease, or riches, or honours. But it promises you that God will be no longer a stranger to you, refuse your converse, withhold his Spirit from you. Your souls shall no longer lie waste and desolate . . . By the remission of sin the bar is removed, and nothing can hinder the Holy Ghost from entering to take possession of your souls as his own temple and dwelling-place.[22]

Remission of sin . . . as it signifies giving a right to future impunity, signifies giving a right to the participation of the Spirit . . . And as it signifies the actual taking off of that punishment, it must connote the actual communication of the Spirit. Therefore, upon that faith which is our entrance into the gospel covenant, the curse which withheld the Spirit is removed, and so we receive the promise of the Spirit by faith (Jer. 31:31, 32; Ps. 51:9–11).[23]

We, therefore, see that this great gift of the Holy Ghost is granted entirely on the Redeemer's account, and by the authority of his office, for the building and inhabiting the desolate temple of God with men.

Thus far we have been considering the temple of God individually taken . . . I now pass on to treat of the external state of the Christian church, and of the whole community of Christians (Eph. 2:20–22). Other foundation none can lay than Jesus Christ (I Cor. 3:11). Yet some are for superstructuring one thing, some another . . . Great differences there have long been, and still are, about setting up the pinnacles and adjoining certain appendicles . . . Some are for garnishing and adorning it in one way, some in another. And too many agitate these little differences with contentious heats and angers . . . Ill-willers look on with pleasure . . . But it is built on a rock, against which the gates of hell can never prevail!

There yet will be a time of so copious an effusion of the Holy Spirit as will invigorate it [the church] afresh, and make it spring up out of its withered state into its primitive liveliness and beauty . . . But before that time there [may] be a day that shall burn as an oven . . . wherein the jealous God shall plead against the Christian church, for its lukewarmness and scandalous coldness in the matter of serious substantial religion . . . no less scandalous heats and fervours about trivial formalities, with just indignation and flames of consuming fire.[24]

We may expect a twofold effusion: of the wrath, and of the Spirit of God. The former to vindicate himself; the other to reform us. Then will this temple no more be termed forsaken . . . Till then, little prosperity is to be hoped for in the Christian church . . . The imperiousness of some and peevishness of others . . . will not let the church, the house of God, be in peace . . . Till those happier days come, wherein Christians shall be of one heart and one way, happy are they that can attain so far to bear one another's yet remaining differences . . . "Lift up the everlasting doors, that the King of glory may come in" . . . Look to Emmanuel.[25]

ELEVEN

❧ THOMAS MANTON ❧

1620—77

Following studies at Oxford, Thomas Manton was ordained to the gospel ministry and succeeded Obadiah Sedgwick as rector of St. Paul's, Covent Garden, a Puritan parish, in 1650. He was involved in the work of the Westminster Assembly, and that of the Savoy Conference. Manton preached before Parliament during the time of Cromwell and the Commonwealth. Nevertheless, he favoured the restoration of the monarchy and was appointed as a royal chaplain by Charles II. Offered the deanery of Rochester on condition of subscription to the Act of Uniformity in 1662, he regarded that offer as a bribe to be declined. His conscientious scruples led to a period of imprisonment. Through his lucid commentaries, however, Manton continues to exercise a ministry across the centuries. In addition to his exposition of James (1651) and the posthumously published work on the Lord's Prayer (1684), he produced a commentary on Jude (1658). These writings are characterized by fidelity to the intent of the sacred writers, and clarity for the benefit of devoted readers.

The Epistle of Jude

The people of God have ever been exercized with two sorts of enemies—persecutors and sectaries: it is hard to say which is worse. When the Christian Church began first to look forth in the world, there were adverse powers without ready to crush it, and Libertines who, like worms bred within the body, sought to devour the entrails and eat out its very bowels. [These] being once turned aside from the truth and the fellowship of the faithful, lost all awe of God, and were given up to sottish judgment to believe all kinds of fables and fancies . . . The spirit and drift of this epistle [Jude] is carried out mainly against this fanatical and libertine party.[1]

Jude is the author of this epistle. He is described as "the servant of Jesus Christ," [indicating] a subserviency to God's will and secret counsels, or instrumentality in the execution of his decrees . . . and pious care to perform God's revealed will . . . [and] designation to any public office for God's glory.

It is royal and kingly to be God's servant . . . and as we have a glorious master, so consider your fellow-servants. The glorified saints and we make but one family . . . When we have such fellow-servants, we should not count our work a slavery and baseness. . . . Learn to value the honour that you have by Christ's service . . . If we would be Christ's, we must do his will. Our relation arises from service (John 12:26).[2]

Whoever is Christ's servant must . . . give himself wholly to the will of Christ . . . Your tongues are not your own to speak what you please, nor your hearts your own to think what you please . . . By virtue of creation you are another's . . . But this is not all. By redemption you are Christ's. "You are bought with a price" (I Cor. 6:20), as the redeemed are bound to serve him that ransomed them . . . Christ has bought us from the worst slavery, and with the greatest price . . . To live as if we were at our own disposal is to defraud Christ of his purchase . . . But now, if we would be his servants, we must be his by voluntary contract and spiritual resignation.[3]

Usually men divide themselves between God and the world; they would give their consciences to Christ, and their hearts to mammon . . . Having given up yourselves to God's service, you must walk as his servants . . . earnestly desire the knowledge of his will, and readily comply with it . . . When God and our lusts or our interests command contrary things, then you are put to the trial whether you are God's servants.[4]

"Many are called, but few are chosen" (Matt. 20:16); that is, outwardly called in the invitation of the word . . . But there is an inward and effectual calling, by the persuasion of the Spirit, or "the voice of the Son of God," which causes life (John 5:25).[5]

God's people are a called people . . . from self to Christ, from sin to holiness, from misery to happiness and glory . . . The main end of a call is to bring Christ and the soul together . . . God speaks to us by conscience, by his works, by benefits, by crosses, but chiefly by his word . . . by the voice of the gospel.[6]

Christ does not call us *because* we are holy, but that we may *become* holy. We must "make our calling and election sure" (II Pet. 1:10), to evidence our election by our calling . . . Election is nothing but God's love and intention to bestow saving grace (Rom. 8:30). Calling is the first and immediate fruit of election (II Thess. 2:13, 14) . . . Calling is the key of the gospel, the plank that is cast out to save a sinking sinner.[7]

God's people, whom he has called out of the world to himself, are a sanctified people . . . To sanctify is to set apart from common use, a setting apart for God . . . separated from the perishing world to be "vessels of honour for the master's use" (II Tim. 2:21) . . . Every sin is a kind of sacrilege, it steals a holy thing away from God . . . To sanctify is to cleanse . . . We all come into the world polluted with the stain of sin, which is purged and done away by degrees, and at death wholly. To be sanctified is more than to be purified; for besides the expulsion of sin, there is an infusion of grace, a disposition wrought clean contrary to what we had before . . . "a new heart and a new spirit" (Ezek. 36:25–27).[8]

The salvation of the people of God is a common salvation . . . common to all believers. They are all chosen by the same grace . . . they have the same Christ . . . are justified by the same righteousness . . . have the same privileges . . . are all under the same rule and direction . . . are in one mystical body.

There are not several ways to heaven, there is but one "common salvation" to all the elect, and one "common faith" as Paul says (Titus 1:4) . . . All the elect are brought to heaven the same way, whether "Jew or Gentile, bond or free." There is a good old way (Jer. 6:16), which, if we miss, we are sure to perish.

You should earnestly contend for the faith that was delivered to the saints . . . The doctrine of faith . . . the word which we believe . . . sound doctrine, such as is necessary to be owned and believed unto salvation, [should be preserved] safe and sound to future ages . . . It is not a thing invented, but given; not discovered by me, but delivered by God himself . . . that we may keep it for posterity . . . The doctrine of salvation was given but *once*, as never to be altered and changed, once for all.

Christ, who has given prophets and apostles to the church to write Scripture, has also given pastors and teachers to open and apply Scripture, so that it might still be delivered to the saints and vindicated when opposed.

There are fundamentals and essentials in religion which challenge the choicest of our care and zeal, that they may be kept entire and without violation; the ignorance of them is damnable, and the denial heretical . . . Christians must have a share in this holy contention [for the faith] by the profession of the truth, whatever it cost . . . Even women may put in a share. They have lives to sacrifice upon the interest of the truth.[9]

Ministers are to contend for the truth, for by their office and station in the church they are captains of the people in this war against Satan . . . It is required of them . . . not only to "exhort by sound doctrine," but to "convince the gainsayers" (Titus 1:9) . . . Ministers must contend partly by preaching, waning, disputing . . . that truth may beat its enemy.[10]

The constant defense of the truth is now a necessity . . . because false teachers . . . had slyly taken up the general name and profession of Christians . . . They crept [into the church] unawares . . . Learn hence to be more watchful in admissions to the church: no perils so great as those occasioned by false brethren . . . It is good to be strict, lest by promiscuous admissions we bring in such a mischief to the church as we cannot easily get rid of.

Be sound in the faith, that you may discern between good and evil . . . You need not only skill, but care and watchfulness.[11]

The gospel yields no freedom to sin, but liberty to serve God. This is its great design. Christ came not to reconcile God and our sins together, but God and our persons, to reconcile our persons and destroy our sins.

In the gospel there is pardon for failings, but not to encourage us to our failings but our duties . . . If we look backward, we are bound in point of gratitude to serve the Lord, being redeemed hereunto by the blood of Jesus; if we look forward, we are encouraged by the hopes of eternal life . . . The great design of the gospel is to make us more like God, and to free us from the slavery of the devil, that we may be better servants and subjects of God . . . "Use not your liberty as an occasion to the flesh" (Gal. 5:13) . . . They that have a mind to fall shall not lack a stone of stumbling; they that will only be feasted with comforts, no wonder if they contract with a spiritual sickness and undo their souls by a misunderstood and misapplied gospel.[12]

Because we all naturally desire liberty, carnal liberty, to be left to our own sway and bent, we catch at anything that tends that way. We would be as gods, lords of our own actions, and so are very apt to dream of an exemption from all kind of law but our own lusts: the seducer's bait was a "promise of liberty" (II Pet. 2:19) . . . We would fain . . . be at our own disposal, to be answerable to none that should call us to an account . . .

As God's patience is abused, so is also his goodness and bounty . . . God's doing all in the covenant of grace is abased to exclude all care of duty. May we not be guilty of this great sin.[13]

Half-truth has filled the world with looseness; when men divide between Christ's comforts and Christ's grace, his priesthood and his royalty, his benefits and his laws, these partial apprehensions spoil all. As to your manner of learning, let it be saving and such as tends to practice. It is not enough to make Christ our teacher by using his word and looking for the direction of his Spirit, and to make the whole counsel of God our lesson; but we must also learn . . . to put off the old man, to put on the new, and not to store the brain with knowledge so much as the heart with grace; for to this end is the gospel given to us.[14]

Christ is denied either by the filthy lifestyle of Christians or else by heretical insinuations striking at his person and natures . . . Who are those that deny his Lordship? They that will not hear his voice . . . that cannot endure his restraints . . . are given up to strong and inordinate desires of liberty, [supposing] and following the bent and sway of their own hearts.

Christ is a prophet to show us our misery, a priest to provide a remedy, a king to instate us in that remedy . . . Christ is the *way* as a priest for by his oblation and intercession we have the boldness to come to God; the *truth* as a prophet; the *life* as a being [who gives] grace and glory (John 14:6).[15]

Christ is denied when men deny his deity or humanity . . . his offices of king, priest, and prophet . . . Christ is denied in practice by apostasy and total revolt from him . . . Men deny Christ when they profess him and walk unworthily . . . Profession of Christianity without answerable practice makes us in worse case than a heathen who is ignorant of Christ and salvation by him . . . This is to deny Christ, when we deny the virtue and power of that religion which he has established, and will not allow it to enter our hearts . . . Well, then, take heed of denying Christ . . . They do not only deny Christ that question his natures or make void his offices, but they that despise his laws, when they do not walk answerably, or contrary.[16]

Murmuring is a great sin . . . it is the scum of discontent, or the vent of impatience, or such bold expostulations and complaints as flow from an exulcerated mind . . . First men mutter and then complain. The heart boils with impatience and then the froth is cast out in passionate speeches and complaints. Humble complaints are not murmurings, else there would be no place for prayer; but bold expostulations are murmurings when we complain rather *of* God than *to* God.[17]

When your hearts storm, look back . . . a good memory is a help to thankfulness . . . All comes to pass by God's providence . . . If the times be bad, what have I done to make them better?[18]

It is not sufficient to be established or grounded in the faith, but we must daily increase and grow more and more therein . . . It is the holy ambition of Christians to be more like God every day . . . None are so knowing but that they may know more . . . Here we are in a state of progress, not of rest and perfection . . . always reaching forth and pressing onward.

To grow in faith is a means to persevere in faith. Man is of an active nature; either he grows better or worse. We shall not keep what we have received if we do not labour to increase in it, as a house begun to be built goes to decay and drops down more and more, if we do not go on to finish it.[19]

Faith is the proper foundation of holiness and good works . . . The faith of Christians is a "most holy faith"; no doctrine has such pure precepts, such high examples, such raised motives, such mysterious enforcements, such blessed rewards, and all to encourage holiness.

In the word of God you have the copy of his holiness . . . An impure life will not suit with a holy faith; you dishonour God and disparage your religion when you walk as heathens. This holy faith is but "kept in pure conscience" (I Tim. 3:9).

Good company preserves and keeps up your warmth and vigour as a remedy against apostasy.[20]

We are kept by God's power, and God's power is triggered by prayer . . . We pray aright when we "pray in the Holy Ghost." This is necessary with respect to acceptance . . . Surely, God's ear will be opened if our hearts be opened . . . Fire from heaven to consume the sacrifice was the solemn token of acceptance heretofore; fire from heaven is the token still, even a holy ardour wrought in us by the Spirit.

Prayer is a work too hard for us; we can babble of ourselves, but we cannot pray without the Holy Ghost; we can put words into prayer, but it is the Spirit who puts affections, without which it is but a little cold prattle and spiritless talk.[21]

The matter of prayer is suggested by the Holy Ghost . . . The direction of the Holy Ghost is necessary, that we may not ask a scorpion instead of a fish, and a stone instead of bread (Rom. 8:27) . . . The Holy Ghost teaches us to ask not only for what is lawful, but what is expedient for us, so that the will of God may have priority over our inclinations.

We come to him with affection . . . with confidence . . . and with reverence. [Consider] the privileges of the saints. God is their Father, willing to hear prayers; Christ is their advocate, willing to present their requests in count; and the Spirit is a notary to indite and draw up their requests for them. Oh, what an encouragement we have to go to the throne of grace![22]

In perseverance, there is a concurrence of our care and diligence (Phil. 2:12, 13) . . . The main work is God's: "He that has begun a good work must perfect it" (Phil. 1:6) . . . But yet there is a concurrence of our care and endeavours . . . We have a power to act and do what is necessary for the preservation of the spiritual life. Well, then, let us not neglect the means. You must not think that God must do all. He does all, indeed, but in us and by us. Idle wishes will do us no good as long as our hands refuse to labour.

We ourselves are prone to . . . a decay of both faith, love, and obedience, which are the three main graces . . . We are assaulted with continual temptations . . . apt to grow secure and negligent . . . Let us make it our care to keep what graces we have gotten.[23]

Flame is soon spent, graces that act most strongly require most influence, as being most subject to abatement. We sooner lose our affections than anything else. Love is a grace we can ill spare; it is the spring and rise of all duties to God and man . . . If we would do anything in the resistance of sin, in keeping the commandments, we cannot spare our love . . . Well, then, watch the more earnestly against the decays and abatements of love.

Sin confessed without remorse . . . prayer made for spiritual blessings without the desire of obtaining . . . hearing without attention . . . singing without any delight or melody of heart—all this is but the just account of a heart declining in the love of God.[24]

Be rooted and grounded in love (Eph. 3:17) . . . a tree that has taken root is in less danger of withering. Increase and grow in love (I Thess. 4:10) . . . Every day you should love sin less, self less, world less, but Christ more and more. Observe the first declinings, for these are causes of all the rest . . . In case of decay, take the advice the Holy Ghost has given you, where three things are required (Rev. 2:5)—consideration, humiliation, reformation . . . It is not enough to know yourselves fallen . . . we must also repent of the decays of love . . . Some may repent that do not reform . . . "Do your first works."[25]

The day of Christ's coming is a day of manifestation. All is now hidden. Christ is hidden, the saints are hidden, their life is hidden (Col. 3:3), their glory is hidden, but then Christ shall appear, and we shall appear with him in glory . . . It is a day of perfection . . . Here we are very weak . . . there is some fruit of sin continued upon the body; but then body and soul are united, and perfectly glorified to praise God in heaven . . . It is a day of congregation, or gathering together. The saints are now scattered, they live in various countries and ages, but then all meet in one assembly and congregation. [We have] an earnest, well-grounded expectation of blessedness to come.[26]

Thoughts are the spies and messengers of hope; it sends them into the promised land to bring the soul tidings from thence . . . By this means we preoccupy and forestall the contentment of what we expect and feast the soul with images and suppositions of what is to come, as if it were already present . . . If we did look upon ourselves as "heirs of the kingdom of heaven" and "co-heirs with Christ" we would think of that happy estate more than we do, and set us in the midst of the glory of the world to come, as if we did see Christ upon his throne, and Paul with his crown of righteousness, and all the blessed in Abraham's bosom.[27]

A believer has eternal life (John 17:3); he begins it here. Hope is called "a lively hope," not only living and lively (I Pet. 1:3) because it quickens the heart, and makes us cheerful and sprightly (Rom. 5:2) . . . Worldly hope is but the dream of a shadow; there is pain and trouble in the expectation, and no satisfaction in the fruition.

The things we look for are holy; it is a great part of our portion in heaven to be free from sin and be consorts of the immaculate Lamb . . . We look for a pure and holy, glorious, and blessed estate, and therefore should begin to purify ourselves (I John 3:3).[28]

The great benefit we have by Christ is eternal life . . . It is an excellent life . . . Rational life is the union of the soul with the body, spiritual life is the union of the soul with Christ, and the life of glory exceeds that in degree . . . It is a happy life . . . not encumbered with miseries as this present life. It is eternal life. This life is but a flower that is soon withered, a vapour that is soon blown over; but this is for ever and ever.

Well, then, let this press you to keep yourselves in the love of God till this happy estate come about.[29]

Reproofs must be managed with compassion and holy grief . . . This is God-like: "He does not afflict willingly, nor grieve the children of men" (Lam. 3:33). There are tears in his eyes when he has a rod in his hand. It is Christ-like: "He wept when he drew near the city" (Luke 19:41). It is suitable to the disposition of God's servants in all ages.

There are three grounds of this holy grief: the dishonour done to God, the harm and destruction men bring upon themselves, and the proneness that is in our nature to the same sin.

Many reproofs are lost, because there is more of passion than compassion in them. It is spiritual cruelty when you can turn a finger in your brother's wound without grief.[30]

Jesus Christ will one day make a solemn presentation of his people to God. There is a three-fold presentation spoken of in Scripture: one made by believers themselves (Rom. 12:1) when we consent to set apart ourselves for God's use . . . [another] by Christ's messengers, who have a charge, and when they have done their work they present us to God (II Cor. 11:12) . . . [and a third] by Christ himself (Eph. 5:27; Col. 1:22). His presenting us to God may be looked upon either as an account of his charge (John 17:4) . . . or as an act of delight and rejoicing in his own success, that all who were given to him are now fit to be settled in their blessed and glorious estate.[31]

The wisdom of God is seen in creation . . . providence . . . and in the methods of his grace: the transactions of God about the salvation of sinners from first to last (Rom. 11:33–36) . . . the overruling of all events to further the eternal blessedness of the saints (Rom. 8:28).

Wherever you are, say "I am where God has set me. God knows what is better for me than I do myself. He who has put all things in their places has put me in this place, and here I will glorify him" (I Cor. 12:20).

To the only wise God, our Saviour; be glory and majesty, dominion and power, now and ever. A gracious heart has such a sense of God's worth and perfection, that it would have all things that are honourable and glorious ascribed to him (Ps. 72:19).[32]

TWELVE

❧ RICHARD BAXTER ❧

1615–91

Though afflicted with poor health, lacking a university education, and ejected from his parish after the passage of the Act of Uniformity, Richard Baxter may be considered one of England's greatest theologians and model pastors. His ministry at Kidderminster showed that instruction in biblical truth could be used by the Spirit of God to change towns as well as individuals for the better. During the civil war, though siding with the parliamentary faction, he advocated fairness and moderation. Baxter, like John Howe, provided leadership for the nonconformists who attended the Savoy Conference. The Reformed Pastor (1656), based on Acts 20:28, had a profound influence on Philip Doddridge, John and Charles Wesley, Thomas Chalmers, and Charles Spurgeon. It continues to serve as an excellent manual of pastoral ministry today. Among his other writings are The Saints' Everlasting Rest (1650) and A Call to the Unconverted (1657).

The Saints' Everlasting Rest

Take God in Christ for your only rest, and fix your heart upon him above all. May the living God, who is the portion and rest of his saints, make our carnal minds so spiritual, and our earthly hearts so heavenly, that loving him and delighting in him may be the work of our lives; and that neither I nor you may ever be turned from this path of life, lest a promise being left us of entering into his rest, we should come short of it, through our own unbelief or negligence . . . The saint's rest is the most happy state of a Christian. It is the perfect endless enjoyment of God by the perfected saints, according to the measure of the capacity to which their souls arrive at death, and both body and soul most fully after the resurrection and final judgment.[1]

One thing contained in heavenly rest is the ceasing from the means of grace. We have obtained the haven, we have done sailing. When the workman receives his wages, it is implied that he has done his work. When we are at our journey's end, we have done with the way . . . There shall be no more prayer because there shall be no more necessity but the full enjoyment of what we have prayed for. Neither shall we need to fast, and watch, and weep any more, being out of the reach of sin and temptation . . . The labourers are called in because the harvest is gathered, the tares burned, and the work finished; the unregenerate past hope, and the saints past fear, for ever.[2]

There is in heavenly rest a perfect freedom from all evils . . . In heaven there is nothing that defiles or is unclean. All *that* remains without. And doubtless there is not such a thing as grief and sorrow known there; nor is there such a thing as a livid face, a languid body, feeble joints, helpless infancy, decrepit age, peccant humours, painful or pining sickness, gripping fears, consuming cares, nor whatever deserves the name evil. We wept and lamented when the world rejoiced; but our sorrow is turned to joy, and our joy shall no man take from us.[3]

Another ingredient of this rest is the highest degree of the saints' personal perfection, both of body and soul . . . The principal part of this rest is our nearest enjoyment of God, the chief good . . . If I should tell a worldling what the holiness and spiritual joys of the saints are on earth, he cannot know because grace cannot be clearly known without grace. How much less could he conceive it, should I tell him of this glory![4]

Be of good cheer, Christian. The time is near when God and you shall be near, and as near as you can desire. You will dwell in his family . . . in his presence. You will be his child, and he your Father. You shall be an heir of his kingdom.[5]

Marvel not, Christian, how it can be eternal life to know God and Jesus Christ. To enjoy God and Christ is eternal life, and the soul's enjoying is in knowing. They that savor only of earth, and consult with flesh, think it a poor happiness to know God. But we know that we are of God, and the whole world lies in wickedness. And we know that the Son of God is come, and has given us an understanding, that we may know him who is true. And we are in him that is true, even in his Son, Jesus Christ. This is the true God, and eternal life.[6]

Christian, though you love as much as you can, you shall be ten thousand times more beloved. The arms of the Son of God were open upon the cross, and an open passage made to his heart by the spear. Will not his arms and heart be open to you in glory?

He that in love wept over old Jerusalem when near its ruin, with what love will he rejoice over the new Jerusalem in her glory? Christian, believe this and think on it: you will be eternally embraced in the arms of that love which was from everlasting and will extend to everlasting . . . That love which was weary, hungry, tempted, scorned, scourged, buffeted, spit upon, crucified, pierced . . . that love will eternally embrace you.[7]

The most glorious coming and appearance of the Son of God may well be reckoned in his people's glory. For their sake he came into the world, suffered, died, rose, ascended. And for their sake it is that he will return. To this end will Christ come again, to receive his people unto himself, that where he is they may be also . . . He forgets not his promise, nor us.

If the heavenly host, for the celebration of his nativity, must praise God, with what shoutings will angels and saints at that day proclaim glory to God, peace and good-will toward men! If a star must lead men from remote parts of the world to come and worship a child in a manger, how will the glory of his next appearing constrain all the world to acknowledge his sovereignty![8]

Another thing that leads to paradise is that great work of Jesus Christ in raising our bodies from the dust and uniting them again unto the soul—a wonderful effect of infinite power and love . . . Look not on the dead bones and dust, and difficulty, but at the promise. Contentedly commit these bodies to a prison that shall not long contain them. Let us lie down in peace and take our rest. It will not be an everlasting night, nor endless sleep . . . Lay down cheerfully this lump of corruption. You shall undoubtedly receive it again in incorruption . . . Triumph now, O Christian, in these promises. You will shortly triumph in their performance . . . rejoice and be glad.[9]

Everyone must give an account of his stewardship. Every talent of time, health, wit, mercies, afflictions, means, warnings, must be reckoned for. The sins of youth, those which they had forgotten, and their secret sins, shall all be laid before angels and men. They shall see the Lord Jesus, whom they neglected and whose word they disobeyed . . . now sitting to judge them . . .

There is no condemnation to them that are in Christ Jesus . . . If our Judge condemn us not, who shall?

What inexpressible joy, that our dear Lord, who loves our souls, and whom our souls love, shall be our Judge. Will a man fear to be judged by his dearest friend?[10]

As Christ is anointed both King and Priest, so under him are his people made to God both kings and priests, to reign and to offer praises for ever. The crown of righteousness, which was reserved for them, shall by the Lord—the righteous Judge—be given them at that day. They have been faithful unto death, and therefore he will give them a crown of life. . . . He prepared the kingdom for us, and then prepared us for the kingdom. This is the preparation of his counsel and decree . . . not only from the promise after Adam's fall, but from eternity.[11]

To be the people of God without regeneration is as impossible as to be the children of men without generation. Seeing we are born God's enemies, we must be new-born to be his sons, or remain enemies still. The greatest reformation of life that can be attained to—without this new life wrought in the soul—may procure our further delusion, but never our salvation.

This new life in the people of God reveals itself by conviction, or a deep sense of divine things. They are convinced of the evil of sin . . . convinced of their own misery by reason of sin . . . convinced of the creature's vanity and insufficiency . . . and of the absolute necessity, the full sufficiency, and perfect excellency of Jesus Christ.[12]

Our aversion from sin, renouncing our idols, and our right receiving Christ, is all but one work which God ever perfects where he begins. At the same time, the will cleaves to God the Father and to Christ . . . To take the Lord for our God is the natural part of the covenant. The supernatural part is to take Christ for our Redeemer . . . Faith accepts him as Saviour and Lord: for in both relations will he be received, or not at all. Faith not only acknowledges his sufferings, and accepts of pardon and glory, but acknowledges his sovereignty and submits to his government and way of salvation.[13]

Has Christ the highest place in your heart and affections?[14]

All things must come to their perfection by degrees. The strongest man must first be a child. The greatest scholar must first begin with the alphabet. The tallest oak was once an acorn. This life is our infancy. Would we be perfect in the womb, or born at full stature? If our rest was here, most of God's providences would be useless . . . If we were happy, innocent, and perfect, what use was there for the glorious work of our sanctification, justification, and future salvation? If we lacked nothing, we would not depend on God so closely, nor call upon him so earnestly.[15]

If Christians would have comforts that will not deceive them, let them make it the great labour of their lives to grow in grace, to strengthen and advance the interest of Christ in their souls, and to weaken and subdue the interest of the flesh. Deceive not yourselves with a persuasion that Christ has done all, and left you nothing to do. To overcome the world, the flesh, and the devil—and, in order to that, to stand always armed upon our watch, and valiantly and patiently to fight it out—is of great importance to our assurance and salvation. Indeed, it is so important, that he who performs it not is no more than a nominal Christian.[16]

God is the saint's treasure and happiness; heaven is the place where they must fully enjoy him. A heart set upon heaven therefore is a heart set upon God. And surely, a heart set upon God, through Christ, is the truest evidence of saving grace . . . Christians, as you would have a proof of your title to glory, labour to get your hearts above. If sin and Satan keep not your affections from thence, they will never be able to keep away your persons.

The noblest of Christians are they whose faces are set most direct for heaven . . . What makes such frozen, uncomfortable Christians, but their living so far from heaven?[17]

God has provided us a crown of glory, and promised to set it shortly on our heads, yet we will not so much as think of it . . . By believing are we "filled with joy and peace," and no longer than we continue believing. It is in hope the saints rejoice, and no longer than they continue hoping. God's Spirit works comfort in us by setting our own spirits at work upon the promises, and raising our thoughts to the place of our comforts . . . He does not kindle our joys while we are idle, or taken up with other things . . . Learn the art of heavenly-mindedness . . . A heart in heaven will be a most excellent preservative against temptations to sin.[18]

The diligent keeping of your hearts in heaven will maintain the vigour of all your graces, and put life into all your duties. The heavenly Christian is the lively Christian . . . We run so slowly, and strive so lazily, because we so little mind the prize.[19]

When others are ready, like Ahab's priests, to "cut themselves" because their sacrifice will not burn, may you breathe the Spirit of Elijah, and in the chariot of contemplation soar aloft till your soul and sacrifice gloriously flame, though the flesh and the world should cast upon them all the water of their opposing enmity.[20]

As Abraham saw Christ's day and rejoiced, so we, in our most forlorn state, see that day when Christ shall give us rest and therein rejoice. I beseech you, Christian, for the honour of the Gospel, and for your soul's comfort, leave not this heavenly art to be learned when in your greatest extremity you have most need to use it. He who with Stephen "sees the glory of God, and Jesus standing on the right hand of God," will comfortably bear the shower of stones. "The joy of the

Lord is our strength," and that joy must be drawn from the place of our joy. If we walk without our strength, how long are we likely to endure?[21]

When a worldly man will talk of nothing but the world, and a politician of state affairs, and a mere scholar of human learning, and a common professor of his duties, the heavenly man will be speaking of heaven, and the strange glory his faith has seen, and our speedy and blessed meeting there. How refreshing and useful are his expressions! How his words pierce and melt the heart, and transform hearers into other men![22]

This is the Christian of the right stamp, and all about him are better because of him . . . For my part, I had rather have the company of a heavenly-minded Christian than that of the most learned disputants or princely commanders.

A soul that does not set its affections on things above disobeys the commands, and loses the most gracious and delightful discoveries of the word of God . . .

As heaven is the perfection of all our mercies, so the promises of it in the Gospel are the very souls of the Gospel . . . It has pleased our Father to open his counsel and let us know the very intent of his heart, that our joy might be full and that we might live as the heirs of such a kingdom . . . And shall we now overlook all? Shall we live in earthly cares and sorrows, and rejoice no more in these discoveries, than if the Lord had never revealed them?[23]

If the Lord of glory can stoop as low as to set his heart on sinful dust, we should easily be persuaded to set our hearts on Christ and glory, and ascend to him in our daily affections who so much condescends to us. Christian, do you not perceive that the heart of God is set upon you, and that he still cares for you with tender love, even when you forget both yourself and him? Is he not following you with daily mercies, moving upon your soul, providing for your body, preserving both? Does he not bear you continually in the arms of love and promise that all shall work together for your good?[24]

Living in any known sin is a great impediment to a heavenly life style. What havoc will this make in your soul! Oh the joys that this has destroyed, the ruin it has made among men's graces, the soul-strengthening duties it has hindered!

Are you a willful neglecter of known duties, either public, private, or secret? Are you a slave to your appetite . . . a proud seeker of your own esteem . . . a peevish and passionate person, ready to take fire at every word or look or supposed slight? Are you a deceiver of others in your dealings, or one who would be rich—right or wrong? If this be your case, I dare say heaven and your soul are very great strangers.[25]

Avoid frequent disputes about lesser truths, and a religion that lies only in opinions . . . He whose religion is all in his opinions will be most frequently and zealously speaking his opinions, and he whose religion lies in the knowledge and love of God and Christ will be most delightfully speaking of that happy time when he shall enjoy them. He is a rare and precious Christian who is skilful to benefit from well-known truths. Therefore let me advise you who aspire after a heavenly life not to spend too much of your thoughts, time, zeal or speech upon disputes that less concern your souls. When hypocrites are feeding on husks or shells, feed on the joys above.[26]

Take heed of a proud and lofty spirit. There is such an antipathy between this sin and God that you will never get your heart near him, nor get him near your heart, as long as this prevails in it. If it cast the angels out of heaven, it must needs keep your heart from heaven . . . It cast our first parents out of paradise . . . and will certainly keep our hearts from paradise . . .

Fellowship with God will keep men low, and that lowliness will promote their fellowship. When a man is used to be much with God and taken up with the study of his glorious attributes, he abhors himself in dust and ashes. And that self-abhorrence is his best preparative to obtain admittance to God again.[27]

Be convinced that heaven is the only treasure and happiness, and labour to know what a treasure and happiness it is. If you do not believe it to be the chief good, you will never set your heart upon it . . . If Eve once supposes she sees more worth in the forbidden fruit than in the love and enjoyment of God, no wonder if it have more of her heart than God. If your judgment once prefer the delights of the flesh before the delights of the presence of God, it is impossible that your heart should be in heaven. As it is ignorance of the emptiness of things below that makes men so overvalue them, so it is ignorance of the high delights above which is the cause that men so little mind them.[28]

What a pity that Christians should ever meet together without some talk of their meeting in heaven or of the way to it, before they part. Pity that so much time is spent in vain conversation and useless disputes, and not a serious word of heaven among them . . . If a Felix will tremble when he hears his judgement powerfully represented, why should not the believer be revived when he hears his eternal rest described? Wicked men can be delighted in talking together of their wickedness. Should not Christians be delighted in talking of Christ, and the heirs of heaven in talking of their inheritance?[29]

The duty of meditation . . . is confessed to be a duty by all, but practically denied by most. Many who make conscience of other duties easily neglect this . . . As digestion turns food into chyle and blood for vigorous health, so meditation turns the truths received and remembered into warm affection, firm resolution, and holy living.

Meditation is the acting of all the powers of the soul . . . The understanding must take in truths, and prepare them for the will and the affections . . . Make meditation a constant standing duty, as you do by hearing, praying, and reading the Scriptures.[30]

This meditation is upon your everlasting rest. I would not have you cast off your other meditations; but surely, as heaven has preeminence in perfection, it should have it also in our meditation . . . This is a walk to Mount Sion: from the kingdoms of this world to the kingdom of saints; from earth to heaven; from time to eternity. It is walking upon sun, moon, and stars, in the garden and paradise of God.[31]

Give this heavenly contemplation a *stated* time . . . Let it be *frequent* as well . . . to prevent a shyness between God and your soul.

Frequent association breeds familiarity, and familiarity increases love and delight.[32]

All things are beautiful and excellent in their season . . . I have always found that the fittest time [to meditate] for myself is the evening, from sunset to twilight . . . The Lord's day is exceedingly seasonable for this exercize. When should we more seasonably contemplate our rest, than on that day of rest which typifies it to us? What fitter time to converse with our Lord than on the Lord's day? What fitter time to ascend to heaven than on that on which he arose from earth and fully triumphed over death and hell? The fittest temper for a true Christian is, like John, to "be in the Spirit on the Lord's day."[33]

Since your enjoyment of God in this contemplation depends much on the capacity and disposition of your heart, seek him here, if ever, with all your soul. Thrust not Christ into the stable and the manger, as if you had better guests for the chief rooms. Say to all your worldly business and thoughts as Christ to his disciples, "Sit here, while I go and pray yonder."[34]

Your heart will be making excursions from your heavenly meditation to other objects . . . Say to your heart, "Would you leave this world, and dwell for ever with Christ in heaven, and not leave it one hour to dwell with Christ in meditation?"[35]

We shall rest from our sin, but not from worship; from suffering and sorrow, but not from joy . . . This is that joy which was procured by sorrow, that crown which was procured by the cross. My Lord wept, that now my tears might be wiped away; he bled, that I might now rejoice; he was forsaken, that I might not now be forsaken; he then died, that I might now live. Oh free mercy, that can exalt so vile a wretch! Free to me, though dear to Christ![36]

I lay down my body in the dust, entrusting not to a grave but to you. Therefore my flesh shall rest in hope, till you shall raise it to the possession of everlasting rest.[37]

❧ JAMES JANEWAY ❧

1 6 3 6 — 7 4

The Janeways were a clerical clan. William, the father, was a minister of the gospel. Son John was influenced by Richard Baxter's The Saints' Everlasting Rest *in coming to conversion, while Abraham was a preacher in London whose Presbyterian principles incurred persecution. James also experienced opposition. The chapel in which he preached was destroyed, and several attempts were made on his life. He died in his thirty-eighth year.*

James Janeway does not deserve the oblivion that shrouds him. His writings include Token for Children, The Saints' Encouragement to Diligence in Christ's Service, Death Unstung: a Funeral Sermon, *and* Heaven Upon Earth: Jesus the Best Friend of Man.

The brief career of James Janeway was well summed up in the oration given by Nathanael Vincent at his funeral: "Christ he loved, in Christ he believed, Christ he preached, Christ he commended."

The treatise entitled Heaven upon Earth *is actually made up of a series of messages calling for a saving knowledge of God. Janeway was profoundly affected by the plague that killed thousands in 1665 and the great fire that destroyed much of London in 1666. He wrote and preached in a time of "political misrule, ecclesiastical oppression, [and] court profligacy," when "Providence spoke in accents of thunder to a nation that seemed to be doomed to destruction."[1] In his epistle to the reader, Janeway said, "The voice of the Lord was not heard, the language of the plague was not understood; wherefore the dreadful Jehovah spake louder and louder, as he did once from Mount Sinai, in fire, flame, and smoke—he rode in a chariot of flaming fire, whilst the bells did ring their own knells as they were tumbling; and it is to be feared, were more melted at the anger of the mighty God, than thousands of hard-hearted men and women were . . . That was a black cloud indeed which no wind could blow over till it fell in such scalding drops."*[2]

Janeway's method may seem tedious to a generation whose attention span is steadily shrinking, but here is passionate pleading flowing from genuine concern. Under Janeway's homiletical flesh there is a solid skeletal structure. His sermons are like a tree—one grand trunk (acquaintance with God), traced through all its branches and twigs (questions, affirmations, appeals, directions), but firmly rooted in the soil of Scripture. Here is one Calvinist whose views on predestination and election in no way blunted or stunted his evangelistic drive.

Heaven upon Earth: Jesus the Best Friend of Man

"Acquaint yourself with him, and be at peace; so shall good come to you" (Job 22:21). They who have improved their experience of things by wisdom, and gathered up the value of man's life by comparing his desire with his enjoyments, his troubles and sorrows with his content and joy, have concluded the worth of life of man to be less than nothing; they have drawn a black line upon the whole, and shut up all in darkness.[3]

We have given our souls into captivity to our bodies, and are gathered up into ourselves, and become deprived of a sufficiency in separation from God . . . We, descending to a lower state than that to which we were made, find nothing but dissatisfaction and emptiness: here we are by nature, and hitherto we have brought ourselves by forsaking God . . . Is there any way whereby we may be delivered from this misery? What way is it? These words, which I have chosen to speak to, do contain the answer to the inquiry.[4]

The doctrine is "Acquaint yourself with him and be at peace." The promise, "So shall good come to you."

The act: Acquaint. The object: God. The first thing that is before us to inquire after is, what this acquaintance with God is. Second, to make clear the duty of man to acquaint himself with God.

Acquaintance with God . . . signifies a full and determinate knowledge of this truth, that there is a God, and so to know him, as to his nature, distinct from all other beings. There is a three-fold knowledge of God: rational, natural, and supernatural—which for its foundation has the word of God.[5]

There is a fourth way of knowing God . . . when God lets out the knowledge of himself . . . as when the sun breaks forth with a bright shining on a cloudy day.[6]

Some resist and stifle that natural knowledge that they have of God (Rom. 1:28) . . . Acquaintance with God implies frequent access to God . . . Under this head, I shall speak first, of that separation that is of the soul from God; secondly, of the return of the soul to God; thirdly, of the abiding of the soul with God.[7]

Of a moral separation from God: there is a great strangeness between our souls and God . . . we reckon ourselves to have little to do with him . . . and that God takes very little regard of us . . . we love not God, and think that God loves not us.[8]

Before we can ever be acquainted with God, the separation must be removed . . . He has set an open door for our return . . . He has revealed his willingness to receive us if we return . . . as a father rejoices to receive a prodigal son that has departed from him . . . While we cleave to our sins, we are separated from God; till we are separated from our sins, we cannot be united to God.[9]

To our acquaintance with God is required an abiding with God . . . If you return to God and continue with God, then shall you be acquainted with him indeed.[10]

There is required to our acquaintance with God an intimate converse with God . . . as those who are of his family.[11]

The communications that are between the soul and God are exceeding transcending all communications between men's acquaintance. Men may communicate their thoughts, their estates, their assistance to one another, but they cannot communicate their life, nor their nature, nor their likeness. But such communications there are between God and the soul that is acquainted with him.[12]

There is likewise required to acquaintance a loving compliance . . . affection . . . As our likeness to God makes us the delight of God, so it makes us delight in God, since the cause of complacency and love is a likeness between the lover and the beloved.[13]

It is the duty of man to acquaint himself with God . . . because therein is the improvement of his highest excellency . . . Now what is this excellency of man? Is it not that he is made in a capacity of knowing God, and enjoying God, and having communion with God? This is the height of his glory.[14]

If we refuse acquaintance with God, it is a slighting of the greatest of all the mercies that God bestows.[15]

It concerns us to acquaint ourselves with God, for without it we are in a necessity of sin and misery.[16]

Is there to be an acquaintance between the soul and God? Let us then stand and wonder at the great condescension of God. This may surprise our souls with an ecstasy of admiration, that God should dwell with man; that the mighty Jehovah should have such respect to the work of his hands.[17]

Is there to be an acquaintance between the soul and God? Then let us learn to make a right judgment of our own excellency; let us judge of ourselves as too high and noble to converse with the base and beggarly world.[18]

By acquaintance with God, we come to have an absolute positive dignity, which is real in our persons, yet still depending on God.[19]

If a man ought to be acquainted with God, then let us all inquire into ourselves, whether we are acquainted with him or no

. . . I know that those that have least acquaintance with God are most apt to neglect this inquiry . . . they are mere strangers to him.[20]

How do things stand between your soul and God?[21]

God, who can in a moment stop your breath and send you into hell, offers to be your friend. If you come in answer to his invitation, well and good, you are happy forever. If not, you will rue the day you were born.[22]

The first head of motives that I shall insist on to enforce this exhortation shall be taken from the nature of the Person that I would have you know.

First, He is the most loving and kind Friend . . . Secondly, He is a most comfortable Friend . . . Thirdly, He is the most able and powerful Friend . . . Fourthly, He is the most active Friend . . . Fifthly, He is the most humble and condescending Friend . . . the most faithful Friend . . . a rich Friend . . . a sympathizing Friend . . . the most patient Friend . . . an honourable Friend . . . a suitable Friend . . . a wise Friend . . . an immortal Friend . . . a present Friend, that is always in all places . . . a soul-Friend . . . a necessary Friend . . . a tried Friend . . . an everlasting Friend . . . One that is willing and desirous to be acquainted with you.[23]

Because man is so wedded to the world and dotes upon his lust, all the arguments that we can use are most commonly unsuccessful. Therefore I shall add one more upon this sort of motives drawn from the qualifications of him whom I would fain have you acquainted with . . . Consider that he is altogether lovely; he is made up of love, goodness, and all excellencies . . . Ask of them that by faith have seen him.[24]

What is the substance of the whole Bible? Does not almost every chapter speak of God's desire to be reconciled to man? Behold, he calls you. He offers you his Son, a kingdom, a crown. Behold, the Father meets, he makes haste, to meet his returning prodigal.[25]

The next head of motives which I shall insist upon, for the enforcing of this duty of acquainting yourselves with God, I shall take from the glorious effect of this acquaintance with God. The first effect of this acquaintance with God is that it makes the soul humble and consequently fits the souls for greater communications from God . . . and do God the greater service . . . When a man begins to be acquainted with God, he begins also to know himself.[26]

The nearer he comes to God, the farther he goes from himself; the more he sees of him and his righteousness, the less he sees of his own.[27]

He does not dissemble with God when he confesses his sin before him.[28]

Another excellent effect of acquaintance with God is that it will make a man fall upon sin in good earnest . . . When he begins to be at peace with God, he commences a war against his adversaries. Friendship with God makes enmity against Satan [and the] unspeakable evil of sin.[29]

Because the grace of God abounds, shall sin abound? God forbid. To argue from mercy to sin is the devil's logic; to argue from mercy to duty is true Christianity.[30]

Happy are they that can always act as in the sight of God . . . Happy are those who, by the thoughts of God, are enraged against sin . . . I will die a thousand deaths before I willingly yield to anything that may be in the least offensive to him whom my soul has such infinite reason to love above the whole world.[31]

When the soul has sweet thoughts of God, it will have sour thoughts of sin. When the soul loves God dearly, it cannot but choose to hate sin entirely. None behold such deformity in sin as those who behold most beauty in God . . . Isaac and Ishmael, the ark and dagon, God and sin, cannot dwell in the same heart . . . Those who walk most closely with God are most tender as to the matter of sin; and those who are less in converse with God are bolder in venturing upon sin, and after it is committed they have less regret.[32]

Another glorious effect of acquaintance with God is, that it makes one to have very low and undervaluing thoughts of the world . . . He reckons that it is better being rich in grace than rich in purse; and that he who lays up for his body, and provides not for his soul, is the greatest fool in the world.[33]

Yet another glorious effect of acquaintance with God is, that it will ease us of all sorrows, or cure all sorrows . . . A saving knowledge of Christ . . . buoys up the soul under the mightiest ways of fear . . . Make sure of this Friend. It is impossible that one with such a Friend should be much daunted. When he hears of wars, when the pestilence rages . . . distress of nations and perplexities, then a child of God may lift up his head with comfort, because his redemption draws near.[34]

It is no unusual thing for a vile unsanctified sinner to leap with a mad confidence into eternity; but he alone has a solid peace who has God for his Friend . . . Would you die joyfully? Why then, you must live holily; get acquainted with God, and then this may be your state.[35]

Another effect of acquaintance with God is, that it will make us honour him more highly. Mere familiarity is far from breeding contempt. Those that are strangers to God see not his worth and excellency, they honour him not, but have the most vile, low, contemptible thoughts of the infinitely glorious majesty.[36]

Still another effect of this acquaintance with God is this: it puts abundance of life and vigour into the soul . . . Those who are most acquainted with God . . . know what it is to present their bodies and souls as a living sacrifice to God through Christ. They understand what it means to be fervent in spirit, serving the Lord . . . Those that are intimately acquainted with God are not so cold, faint, and dull in the service of God as others.[37]

Another excellent effect of this acquaintance with God is, it will make a man patient under all the dispensations of God's providence, in all conditions to be content, in quietness to possess his spirit . . . Though all the world were his enemies, yet as long as Christ was his Friend he does not care.[38]

Acquaintance with God will make a man wise . . . more wise than the great sages and grand politicians of the world . . . able to know right from wrong.[39]

This acquaintance with God . . . will make a man rich. As soon as anyone is acquainted with God, he is set in a thriving way. [Impoverished and indebted through] the serpent, that great cheater, [he is bailed out by Christ]. Through the kindness of Christ, the great Creditor had patience, and offers to make up the business, and to compound on better terms than the sinner could possibly expect. Christ undertakes to heal the infinite breach, to bring God and man acquainted, to set him up again if he will but accept the gracious terms of agreement. Thus, undone man, that was before in a beggarly condition, upon his return to God, is set in a better way than ever.[40]

Another glorious effect of acquaintance with God is, that it makes a man like God . . . Company is of an assimilating nature. He that before was unholy, and like the devil, by conversion to God and converse with him is made holy like God . . . A full and perfect conformity and likeness to God is the very glory of glory . . . Be acquainted with him, and you shall be like him. Keep much in his company by faith, secret prayer, and meditation, and you will be more holy, divine, and spiritual. The last effect of this acquaintance with God: it will make a man better, far more excellent in all states and relations. All his friends will have the better life with him, the whole family . . . will fare the better for him.[41]

How sweet and amiable does acquaintance with God make a man! How ready to heal divisions! How full of goodness and charity! How ready to do good unto all, but especially to those that be of the household of faith! How compassionate and tender-hearted! How ready to provoke others to love and good works: so that the whole parish lives the quieter . . . This is the man who adorns the gospel. This is the Christian who makes credible his profession. This is what it means to be intimately acquainted with God.[42]

The next head of motives to enforce this exhortation might be taken from the danger of not being acquainted with God . . . How can I stand looking upon men and women that are about to murder their own souls, and forbear crying out? How can I endure seeing poor creatures running with all the speed they can to that dismal place from whence there is no redemption?[43]

If you will not be acquainted with God, you shall be acquainted with the devil, and know whose company is best by woeful experience. If you will not believe his word, you shall feel his sword. If his kindness and goodness will not melt you, his power and justice shall break you.[44]

Speak quickly! What will you do? Turn, or burn. Repent, or die![45]

How just must their condemnation be, who are offered salvation so often, and refuse it . . . who might have God for their Friend, and had rather have him for their Enemy![46]

The next head of motives by which I might enforce this duty of acquaintance with God may be taken from the examples of them who made all the friends they can get acquainted with God. Behold a cloud of witnesses . . . brave worthies . . . the wonders of the world, the non-suches of their age . . . a pattern for future generations.[47]

I might also insist on another head of motives, which is named in the text: "Acquaint yourself now with him, and you shall be at peace." Though there be nothing but war on every side, you shall have peace . . . that passes all understanding . . . a well-grounded peace [resulting] from the sense of pardon of sin, and reconciliation with God, through the blood of Christ.[48]

Are the things which you have heard true, or are they not? Do not the Scriptures speak the same things which I do? Dare you say that the Word of Truth is false?[49]

Are these things of weight and importance, or are they not? If acquaintance with God, the happiness or misery of a soul, your making or undoing forever be inconsiderable things, then what are great things?[50]

What do you mean then, to treat such things . . . with so much indifference and coldness?[51]

Do you believe that you can find a better friend than God? Can you mend yourself anywhere else?[52]

Do you think that this world will last always with you? What do you think will become of you . . . if you should die without the knowledge of God?[53]

Direction I: If you would be acquainted with God, labour to get a thorough sense of your great estrangement from him, and of the danger of such an estrangement.[54]

Direction II: Get an humble heart . . . humility is an excellent grace, it makes the soul fit for the richest enjoyments of God, and to do God the greatest service.[55]

Direction III: If you would be acquainted with God, you must visit him often . . . knock at his door . . . wait for him . . . through solemn meditation, secret prayer, fasting, communion with the saints, and the Lord's Supper.[56]

Direction IV: If you would get acquaintance with God, get Christ along with you, when you go to God . . . There is no name under heaven by which we can be saved, but by the name of Christ; and whosoever comes to the Father by him, he will in no wise case out . . . Apart from Christ, God is a consuming fire. There is but one Mediator . . . but one Advocate with the Father, Jesus Christ the righteous . . . The righteousness of Christ is that wedding garment in which we may sit at the King's table, and are welcome . . . When any come to God without Christ, they come like Simon Magus, with their own money in their hand to buy a great commodity, which is not to be purchased with such kind of coin.[57]

Direction V: If you would be acquainted with God, come where he is wont to be, frequent his house, lie always at the doors of wisdom, engage much in his ordinances.[58]

Direction VI: If you would be acquainted with God, you must get acquainted with some of his friends; and they will do all they can—and be glad of it, too—to help you to be acquainted with him . . . If you would be brought to the knowledge of God, go speedily to them that know him well . . . Get acquainted with some warm, rare, experienced Christian.[59]

Direction VII: If you would be acquainted with God, entertain all the messengers he kindly sends you. When God calls, answer.[60]

Direction VIII: Seek this acquaintance most earnestly . . . Strive to enter in at the narrow gate . . . You must grasp Christ, as a man that is drowning would grasp anything that is thrown out to save him.[61]

Direction IX: If you would be acquainted with God, be much in expostulating the case with God, in urging those arguments which the Scripture affords you in such a case. Take words with you, and come to the Lord, and spread your requests before him.[62]

Direction X: If you would be acquainted with God, look after it speedily; defer not a moment . . . "Acquaint yourself with him *now*." "Remember *now* your Creator." "Seek the Lord while he may be found, and call upon him while he is near."[63]

Direction XI: If you would be acquainted with God, take heed of those things which keep God and man at a distance, and make the Lord displeased with us . . . Take heed of pride . . . of a worldly mind . . . of hypocrisy . . . of being acquainted with wicked company . . . of unbelief . . . of sensuality.[64]

Direction XII: If you would be acquainted with God, resolvedly and freely give yourself up to him, and enter in a most solemn covenant with him . . . after a deliberate consideration of the terms of this covenant, and after a thorough search of your own heart . . . Rely on his promise of grace and strength whereby you may be enabled to perform your promise . . . Resolve to be faithful.[65]

And now my work is done, I must leave you; and whether I shall ever speak to you, or see you, or write to you again while the world stands, I know not. My body is frail, and I am a poor dying man, and before long, my mouth will be stopped . . . and yours, too . . . I have set life and death before you . . . I have stayed a great while for an answer . . . You must either speedily come in upon the invitation, and close with those gracious invitations that are made to you, or you . . . must cast yourself away. . . . Seek the Lord while he may be found, and with all possible speed, seriousness, and gratitude, accept of his kindness while you may.[66]

❧ EPILOGUE ❧

According to the empirical philosopher John Locke, whose essays prepared the way for the development of deism in the eighteenth century, the Act of Uniformity "was fatal to our Church and religion, in throwing out a very great number of worthy, learned, pious, and orthodox divines."[1] And the Scottish skeptic David Hume, no friend to Christianity, recognized the costly contribution of the ejected dissenters to the nation's life when he wrote, "To the Puritans are the British Constitution and people indebted for the preservation of the precious spark of liberty, when it was in danger of being extinguished."[2]

One wonders what might have happened if the political and ecclesiastical power structure in seventeenth-century Britain would have shown a catholicity that allowed for diversity on matters that were not of the essence of the gospel—or, if the two thousand ministers who faced ejection would have been more flexible on things neither commanded nor condemned in Holy Scripture, so that they could continue to shepherd their flocks within the national church.

When we move from wondering what might have been to what actually happened, we may learn several valuable lessons: that tradition, even when drawn from the church fathers or the theologians of the Reformation, must be compared with Scripture for confirmation or correction; that Episcopal, Presbyterian, and congregational forms of church government each find some support in the New Testament; that we must earnestly seek the peace *and* purity of the church, speaking the truth in love; that the unique headship of Christ over the church precludes the interference of the state in matters of worship, doctrine, and spiritual discipline; that congregational renewal is possible only when there is personal regeneration and sanctification; and that we are dependent on the grace of God to reach the glorious goal of likeness to Christ.

In the final analysis, what matters most is a daring nonconformity to this present evil age, and complete conformity to God's beloved Son. Justification by grace through faith in Christ alone is a vital aspect of the Reformed faith. But, as the Puritans have emphasized, it should never be severed from self-examination, the crucifixion of the old nature, a diligent use of the means of grace, and growth in godliness. The Christian life is not only a pilgrimage in the direction of the Celestial City. It is a warfare against the world, the flesh, and the Devil—but a warfare that is waged in the confidence that we are more than conquerors through him who loved us.

❧ NOTES ❧

INTRODUCTION

1. T. B. Macauly, *The History of England*, 2 vols. (New York: Harper & Brothers, 1849), 1:76.

2. F. J. Bremer, "Puritanism," in *The Encyclopedia of Religion*, ed. Mircea Eliade, 16 vols. (New York: Macmillan, 1987), 12:104.

3. Ibid.

4. James I. Packer, *A Quest for Godliness: The Puritan Vision of the Christian Life* (Wheaton, Ill.: Crossway, 1990), 11.

5. D. Martyn Lloyd-Jones, *The Puritans: Their Origins and Successors* (Edinburgh: Banner of Truth, 1987), 11.

6. Packer, *Quest for Godliness*, 28.

7. R. F. Lovelace, *Dynamics of Spiritual Life: An Evangelical Theology of Renewal* (Downers Grove, Ill.: InterVarsity Press, 1979), 43.

CHAPTER 1: STEPHEN CHARNOCK

1. Stephen Charnock, *The Existence and Attributes of God* (reprint, Evansville, Ind.: Sovereign Grace Book Club, 1958), 11–13.

2. Ibid., 14.

3. Ibid., 15–17.

4. Ibid., 67.

5. Ibid., 69–70.

6. Ibid., 72–73.

7. Ibid., 74.

8. Ibid., 103–4.

9. Ibid., 111–12, 126–27.

10. Ibid., 131.

11. Ibid., 136.

12. Ibid., 143.

13. Ibid., 147–50.

14. Ibid., 174–75, 179–80.

15. Ibid., 183–84.

16. Ibid., 185, 195–99.

17. Ibid., 204.

18. Ibid., 208.

19. Ibid., 213.

20. Ibid., 219.

21. Ibid., 227.

22. Ibid., 232.

23. Ibid., 249.

24. Ibid., 266.

25. Ibid., 279, 349.

26. Ibid., 362–63.

27. Ibid., 364.

28. Ibid., 376–77.

29. Ibid., 383–84, 390–91.

30. Ibid., 403.

31. Ibid., 448–49.

32. Ibid., 452.

33. Ibid., 462–63, 466–67.

34. Ibid., 471.

35. Ibid., 514.

36. Ibid., 517, 522.

37. Ibid., 535.

38. Ibid., 541.

39. Ibid., 556, 563.

40. Ibid., 571–72.

41. Ibid., 575–76.

42. Ibid., 581–82.

43. Ibid., 583–84.

44. Ibid., 599.

45. Ibid., 600–602.

46. Ibid., 603.

47. Ibid., 604–5.

48 Ibid., 622.

49. Ibid., 624–25, 629.

50. Ibid., 659, 663–64.

51. Ibid., 665, 676.

52. Ibid., 763–64, 770–71.

53. Ibid., 802.

CHAPTER 2: ROBERT LEIGHTON

1. *The Works of Robert Leighton* (London: Nelson & Sons, 1853), on I Peter 1:1.

2. Ibid.

3. Ibid., I Peter 1:2.

4. Ibid.

5. Ibid.

6. Ibid.

7. Ibid., I Peter 1:3, 4.

8. Ibid., I Peter 1:5.

9. Ibid.

10. Ibid., I Peter 1:6.

11. Ibid., I Peter 1:7.

12. Ibid., I Peter 1:16.

13. Ibid., I Peter 1:22.

14. Ibid., I Peter 1:23, 24.

15. Ibid., I Peter 2:1, 2.

16. Ibid.

17. Ibid.

18. Ibid., I Peter 2:6.

19. Ibid., I Peter 2:10.

20. Ibid., I Peter 2:11.

21. Ibid., I Peter 2:12.

22. Ibid., I Peter 2:17.

23. Ibid., I Peter 2:23, 24.

24. Ibid., I Peter 3:7.

25. Ibid., I Peter 3:10.

26. Ibid., I Peter 3:12.

27. Ibid., I Peter 3:15.

28. Ibid., I Peter 3:16.

29. Ibid., I Peter 4:1–3.

30. Ibid., I Peter 4:8.

31. Ibid.

32. Ibid.

33. Ibid., I Peter 4:12.

34. Ibid., I Peter 5:10.

CHAPTER 3: RICHARD SIBBES

1. J. S. Coolidge, *The Pauline Renaissance in England: Puritanism and the Bible* (Oxford: Clarendon Press, 1970), 147 n. 11.

2. *The Complete Works of Richard Sibbes*, vol. 1, *The Description of Christ* (Edinburgh: James Nichol, 1862), 3.

3. Ibid., 8.

4. Ibid., 8–9.

5. Ibid., 10.

6. Ibid., 12.

7. Ibid.

8. Ibid., 13.

9. Ibid.

10. Ibid., 14.

11. Ibid.

12. Ibid., 16.

13. Ibid.

14. Ibid.

15. Ibid., 17.

16. Ibid., 23–24.

17. Ibid., 24.

18. Ibid., 25.

19. Ibid., 28.

20. *The Bruised Reed*, 37–38.

21. Ibid., 42, 43.

22. Ibid., 44.

23. Ibid., 45.

24. Ibid., 46.

25. Ibid., 49, 51.

26. Ibid., 57.

27. Ibid., 58.

28. Ibid., 60.

29. Ibid., 71.

30. Ibid., 76.

31. Ibid., 79.

32. Ibid., 80.

33. Ibid.

34. Ibid., 83.

35. Ibid., 84.

36. Ibid.

37. Ibid., 85.

38. Ibid.

39. Ibid., 86.

40. Ibid.

41. Ibid., 87.

42. Ibid., 90.

43. Ibid., 92.

44. Ibid., 99.

CHAPTER 4: THOMAS WATSON

1. Thomas Watson, *Practical Divinity: The Lord's Prayer* (Philadelphia: Thomas Wardle, 1833), 381.

2. Ibid., 382.

3. Ibid.

4. Ibid., 383.

5. Ibid., 386, 389, 399.

6. Ibid., 403.

7. Ibid., 406.

8. Ibid., 406–8.

9. Ibid., 417, 420.

10. Ibid., 420–22.

11. Ibid., 426, 428.

12. Ibid., 444–45.

13. Ibid., 446.

14. Ibid., 482–83.

15. Ibid., 483–84.

16. Ibid., 485.

17. Ibid., 486.

18. Ibid., 489–90.

19. Ibid., 491.

20. Ibid., 492.

21. Ibid., 493.

22. Ibid., 494.

23. Ibid., 511–12.

24. Ibid., 512.

25. Ibid., 513.

26. Ibid., 513–14.

27. Ibid., 514–15.

28. Ibid., 515.

29. Ibid., 521–22.

30. Ibid., 522–23.

31. Ibid., 523.

32. Ibid., 524–25.

33. Ibid., 526.

34. Ibid., 527.

35. Ibid., 551.

36. Ibid., 555.

37. Ibid.

38. Ibid., 556.

39. Ibid., 556–58.

40. Ibid., 573.

41. Ibid., 584–85.

42. Ibid., 585.

43. Ibid., 596–97.

44. Ibid., 604.

CHAPTER 5: JOHN OWEN

1. *The Works of John Owen*, ed. W. H. Goold, vol. 3, *Discourse on the Holy Spirit* (Edinburgh: Johnstone & Hunter, 1852), 23.

2. Ibid., 25.

3. Ibid., 27.

4. Ibid., 35–36.

5. Ibid., 44.

6. Ibid., 133.

7. Ibid., 143.

8. Ibid., 157.

9. Ibid., 159.

10. Ibid., 162.

11. Ibid., 168, 171, 174.

12. Ibid., 181.

13. Ibid., 183.

14. Ibid., 192.

15. Ibid., 195–96.

16. Ibid., 204.

17. Ibid., 207–8.

18, Ibid., 216.

19. Ibid., 219.

20. Ibid., 222–23.

21. Ibid., 282.

22. Ibid., 292.

23. Ibid., 299.

24. Ibid., 303.

25. Ibid., 324.

26. Ibid., 368.

27. Ibid., 369.

28. Ibid., 370.

29. Ibid., 374.

30. Ibid., 386.

31. Ibid., 387.

32. Ibid., 397.

33. Ibid., 400.

34. Ibid., 429–30.

35. Ibid., 436–37.

36. Ibid., 437.

37. Ibid., 438, 443.

38. Ibid., 468–69.

39. Ibid., 469–70.

40. Ibid., 482.

41. Ibid., 493–94.

42. Ibid., 504.

43. Ibid., 506.

44. Ibid., 508.

45. Ibid., 510–11.

46. Ibid., 513.

47. Ibid., 538.

48. Ibid., 544–45.

49. Ibid., 648–49.

CHAPTER 6: WILLIAM GOUGE

1. *The Works of William Gouge*, 2 vols. (London: John Beale, 1627), 2:1.

2. Ibid., 2.

3. Ibid., 3–4.

4. Ibid., 5.

5. Ibid., 8.

6. Ibid., 18.

7. Ibid., 18–19.

8. Ibid., 20.

9. Ibid., 20–21.

10. Ibid., 22.

11. Ibid., 24.

12. Ibid., 24, 26.

13. Ibid., 27.

14. Ibid., 28.

15. Ibid.

16. Ibid., 31.

17. Ibid., 32.

18. Ibid., 33.

19. Ibid., 46–47.

20. Ibid., 47.

21. Ibid., 50.

22. Ibid., 52.

23. Ibid., 58–59.

24. Ibid., 59–60.

25. Ibid., 71.

26. Ibid., 122.

27. Ibid., 138.

28. Ibid., 144.

29. Ibid., 245.

30. Ibid., 272.

31. Ibid., 302–3.

CHAPTER 7: HENRY SMITH

1. John Brown, *Puritan Preaching in England* (London: Hodder & Stoughton, 1900), 84.

2. A. F. Herr, *The Elizabethan Sermon* (New York: Octagon Books, 1961), 28.

3. *The Sermons of Mr. Henry Smith* (London, 1675), 257–58.

4. Ibid., 259.

5. Ibid., 260–61.

6. Ibid., 268.

7. Ibid., 269–70.

8. Ibid., 271.

9. Ibid., 272.

10. Ibid., 275.

11. Ibid., 365.

12. Ibid., 367.

13. Ibid., 368–69.

14. Ibid., 372–73.

15. Ibid., 374.

16. Ibid., 387.

17. Ibid., 388.

18. Ibid.

19. Ibid., 391, 394.

20. Ibid., 421.

21. Ibid., 422–23.

22. Ibid., 424–25.

23. Ibid., 426–27.

24. Ibid., 428–29.

25. Ibid., 431–32.

26. Ibid., 434–35.

27. Ibid., 438.

28. Ibid., 198.

29. Ibid., 199.

30. Ibid., 200.

31. Ibid., 203–4.

32. Ibid., 217–20.

33. Ibid., 221–22.

34. Ibid., 225.

35. Ibid., 229–30.

36. Ibid., 231–32.

37. Ibid., 235, 242.

38. Ibid., 317.

39. Ibid., 318.

40. Ibid.

41. Ibid., 320.

42. Ibid., 321.

43. Ibid., 322.

44. Ibid., 322–23.

45. Ibid., 326.

46. Ibid., 330.

47. Ibid., 112.

48. Ibid., 114.

49. Ibid., 115–16.

50. Ibid., 118.

51. Ibid., 119–20.

52. Ibid., 121–22.

53. *Three Sermons Made by Henry Smith* (London, 1673, 1675), 3–4.

54. Ibid., 5.

55. Ibid., 6–7.

56. Ibid., 9–10.

CHAPTER 8: JOHN BUNYAN

1. J. R. Knott, *The Sword of the Spirit: Puritan Responses to the Bible* (Chicago: University of Chicago Press, 1980), 131.

2. *The Complete Works of John Bunyan,* ed. J. P. Gulliver (Philadelphia: Bradley & Garretson, 1878), 323.

3. Ibid., 325.

4. Ibid., 326.

5. Ibid., 328.

6. Ibid., 329.

7. Ibid., 330.

8. Ibid., 331.

9. Ibid., 331–32.

10. Ibid., 332–33.

11. Ibid., 333–34.

12. Ibid., 334–35.

13. Ibid., 325–26.

14. Ibid., 336–37.

15. Ibid., 337.

16. Ibid., 338.

17. Ibid., 339.

18. Ibid., 340.

19. Ibid., 343.

20. Ibid.

21. Ibid., 341.

22. Ibid., 347.

23. Ibid., 348.

24. Ibid., 352.

25. Ibid., 353.

26. Ibid., 354–55.

27. Ibid., 359.

28. Ibid., 360–61.

29. Ibid., 361–62.

30. Ibid., 366.

31. Ibid., 815.

32. Ibid., 818–19.

33. Ibid., 820–21.

34. Ibid., 821–22.

35. Ibid., 822–23.

36. Ibid., 823.

37. Ibid., 824.

CHAPTER 9: WILLIAM GURNALL

1. William Gurnall, *The Christian in Complete Armour*, 2 vols. (reprint, London: Banner of Truth, 1964), 1:2–3.

2. Ibid., 4.

3. Ibid., 12.

4. Ibid., 14–15.

5. Ibid., 16.

6. Ibid., 18–19.

7. Ibid., 24.

8. Ibid., 25, 29.

9. Ibid., 45.

10. Ibid., 58, 64.

11. Ibid., 71, 85.

12. Ibid., 94–95, 99.

13. Ibid., 100.

14. Ibid., 103.

15. Ibid., 121.

16. Ibid., 257.

17. Ibid., 258–59.

18. Ibid., 270–71, 274.

19. Ibid., 275.

20. Ibid., 291.

21. Ibid., 292–93.

22. Ibid., 301.

23. Ibid., 395.

24. Ibid., 387–88.

25. Ibid., 402–3.

26. Ibid., 406–7.

27. Ibid., 407–8.

28. Ibid., 409.

29. Ibid., 410.

30. Ibid., 412–13.

31. Ibid., 421–22.

32. Ibid., 422–23.

33. Ibid., 479–80.

34. Ibid., 483.

35. Ibid., 491–92.

36. Ibid., 494.

37. Ibid., 2:8–9.

38. Ibid., 9.

39. Ibid., 10.

40. Ibid., 124, 129.

41. Ibid., 130–31.

42. Ibid., 132–33.

43. Ibid., 194–95.

44. Ibid., 199–200.

45. Ibid., 210.

46. Ibid., 215–16.

47. Ibid., 219–20.

48. Ibid., 236.

49. Ibid., 289.

50. Ibid., 299–300.

51. Ibid., 305.

52. Ibid., 338–40.

CHAPTER 10: JOHN HOWE

1. *The Works of the Rev. John Howe*, 2 vols. (New York: J. P. Haven, 1835), 1:67–68.

2. Ibid., 70.

3. Ibid., 71.

4. Ibid., 76.

5. Ibid., 77.

6. Ibid., 78.

7. Ibid., 79.

8. Ibid., 83.

9. Ibid., 97.

10. Ibid., 98.

11. Ibid., 99.

12. Ibid., 99–100.

13. Ibid., 100.

14. Ibid., 101.

15. Ibid., 102.

16. Ibid.

17. Ibid., 105.

18. Ibid., 106.

19. Ibid., 107.

20. Ibid., 108.

21. Ibid., 109.

22. Ibid., 110.

23. Ibid., 110–11.

24. Ibid., 111.

25. Ibid., 112–13.

CHAPTER 11: THOMAS MANTON

1. Thomas Manton, *An Exposition on the Epistle of Jude* (reprint, London: Banner of Truth, 1958), 6–7.

2. Jude 1.

3. Ibid.

4. Ibid.

5. Ibid.

6. Ibid.

7. Ibid.

8. Ibid.

9. Jude 3.

10. Jude 4.

11. Ibid.

12. Ibid.

13. Ibid.

14. Ibid.

15. Ibid.

16. Ibid.

17. Jude 16.

18. Ibid.

19. Jude 20.

20. Ibid.

21. Ibid.

22. Ibid.

23. Jude 21.

24. Ibid.

25. Ibid.

26. Ibid.

27. Ibid.

28. Ibid.

29. Ibid.

30. Jude 22, 23.

31. Jude 24.

32. Jude 25.

CHAPTER 12: RICHARD BAXTER

1. Richard Baxter, *The Saints' Everlasting Rest*, abridged by Benjamin Fawcett (New York: American Tract Society, 1824), 21.

2. Ibid., 26.

3. Ibid., 26–27.

4. Ibid., 28.

5. Ibid., 31.

6. Ibid., 35.

7. Ibid., 38.

8. Ibid., 47.

9. Ibid., 50.

10. Ibid., 50–51.

11. Ibid., 55, 57.

12. Ibid., 85–86.

13. Ibid., 91–92.

14. Ibid., 95.

15. Ibid., 101.

16. Ibid., 209.

17. Ibid., 276–77.

18. Ibid., 279–80.

19. Ibid., 285–86.

20. Ibid., 287.

21. Ibid., 290–91.

22. Ibid., 291–92.

23. Ibid., 294–95.

24. Ibid., 296.

25. Ibid., 303–4.

26. Ibid., 309–10.

27. Ibid., 311.

28. Ibid., 318–19.

29. Ibid., 323.

30. Ibid., 334–35.

31. Ibid., 337.

32. Ibid., 338–39.

33. Ibid., 341–42.

34. Ibid., 350.

35. Ibid., 403.

36. Ibid., 438.

37. Ibid.

CHAPTER 13: JAMES JANEWAY

1. F. A. Cox, in *Heaven upon Earth, or Jesus the Best Friend of Man* (London: Thomas Nelson, 1847), 22.

2. Ibid., 26.

3. Ibid., 37.

4. Ibid., 38.

5. Ibid., 40–41.

6. Ibid., 41.

7. Ibid., 41–42.

8. Ibid., 42.

9. Ibid., 43–44.

10. Ibid., 44.

11. Ibid., 46.

12. Ibid., 48.

13. Ibid., 50.

14. Ibid., 51, 55.

15. Ibid., 57.

16. Ibid., 58.

17. Ibid., 62.

18. Ibid., 64.

19. Ibid., 70.

20. Ibid., 71–72, 74.

21. Ibid., 78.

22. Ibid., 82.

23. Ibid., 82–156.

24. Ibid., 156.

25. Ibid., 159.

26. Ibid., 162–63.

27. Ibid., 164.

28. Ibid., 166.

29. Ibid., 166–67.

30. Ibid., 168–69.

31. Ibid., 170–71.

32. Ibid., 172–73.

33. Ibid., 172, 176.

34. Ibid., 179–80.

35. Ibid., 182–83.

36. Ibid., 187.

37. Ibid., 190.

38. Ibid., 193.

39. Ibid., 195.

40. Ibid., 198.

41. Ibid., 200–201.

42. Ibid., 203.

43. Ibid., 204.

44. Ibid., 205–6.

45. Ibid., 211.

46. Ibid.

47. Ibid., 211–12.

48. Ibid., 215–16.

49. Ibid., 226.

50. Ibid., 228.

51. Ibid., 229.

52. Ibid., 230.

53. Ibid., 231.

54. Ibid., 239.

55. Ibid., 249.

56. Ibid., 252.

57. Ibid., 264–65.

58. Ibid., 267.

59. Ibid., 269–70.

60. Ibid., 274.

61. Ibid., 275–76.

62. Ibid., 280–84.

63. Ibid., 282.

64. Ibid., 288, 294.

65. Ibid., 295.

66. Ibid., 298–99.

EPILOGUE

1. M. Caston, *Independency in Bristol* (London: Ward, 1860), 15.

2. Ibid., 9.

❧ BIBLIOGRAPHY ❧

Baxter, Richard. *The Saints' Everlasting Rest*. Abridged by Benjamin Fawcett. New York: American Tract Society, 1824.

Brevard, I. "Puritan Theology," in *New Dictionary of Theology*. Edited by Ferguson, Wright, Packer. Downers Grove, Ill.: Inter-Varsity Press, 1988.

Brown, John. *Puritan Preaching in England*. London: Hodder & Stoughton, 1900.

Bunyan, John. *The Complete Works of John Bunyan*. Edited by J. P. Gulliver. Philadelphia: Bradley & Garretson, 1878.

Caston, M. *Independency in Bristol*. London: Ward, 1860.

Charnock, Stephen. *The Existence and Attributes of God*. Reprint, Evansville, Ind.: Sovereign Grace Book Club, 1958.

Collinson, Patrick. *The Elizabethan Puritan Movement*. Berkeley, Calif.: University of California Press, 1967.

Coolidge, J. S. *The Pauline Renaissance in England: Puritanism, and the Bible*. Oxford: Clarendon Press, 1970.

The Encyclopedia of Religion. Edited by Mircea Eliade. New York: Macmillan, 1987.

Erickson & Havran. *Readings in English History*. New York: Charles Scribner's Sons, 1967.

Gouge, William. *The Works of William Gouge*. 2 vols. London: John Beale, 1627.

Gurnall, William. *The Christian in Complete Armour*. 2 vols. Reprint, London: Banner of Truth, 1964.

Herr, A. F. *The Elizabethan Sermon*. New York: Octagon Books, 1961.

Hill, Christopher. *A Tinker and a Poor Man: John Bunyan and His Church, 1628–1688*. New York: Knopf, 1989.

Howe, John. *The Works of the Rev. John Howe.* 2 vols. New York: J. P. Haven, 1835.

Janeway, James. *Heaven upon Earth, or Jesus the Best Friend of Man.* London: Thomas Nelson, 1847.

Knott, J. R. *The Sword of the Spirit: Puritan Responses to the Bible.* Chicago: University of Chicago Press, 1980.

Lake, Peter. *Anglicans and Puritans?* London: Unwin Hyman, 1988.

Leighton, Robert. *The Works of Robert Leighton.* London: Nelson & Sons, 1853.

Liu, Tai. *Discord in Zion: The Puritan Divines and the Puritan Revolution, 1640–1660.* The Hague: Martinus Nijhoff, 1973.

———. *Puritan London.* Newark, Del.: University of Delaware Press, 1986.

Lloyd-Jones, D. M. *The Puritans: Their Origins and Successors.* Edinburgh: Banner of Truth, 1987.

Loane, Marcus L. *Makers of Puritan History.* Grand Rapids: Baker, 1980.

Lovelace, R. F. *Dynamics of Spiritual Life: An Evangelical Theology of Renewal.* Downers Grove, Ill.: InterVarsity Press, 1979.

Manton, Thomas. *An Exposition on the Epistle of Jude.* Reprint, London: Banner of Truth, 1958.

Martin, Hugh. *Puritanism and Richard Baxter.* London: SCM Press, 1954.

McGee, J. S. *The Godly Man in Stuart England: 1620–1670.* New Haven, Conn.: Yale University Press, 1976.

Miller, Perry, ed. *The American Puritans: Their Prose and Poetry.* Garden City, N.Y.: Doubleday, 1956.

New, J. F. H. *Anglican and Puritan: The Basis of Their Opposition, 1558–1640.* Stanford, Calif.: Stanford University Press, 1964.

The New International Dictionary of the Christian Church. Rev. ed. J. D. Douglas. Zondervan, Grand Rapids, 1978.

The New Schaff-Herzog Encyclopedia of Religious Knowledge. Edited by S. M. Jackson. New York: Funk & Wagnalls, 1912.

Owen, John. *The Works of John Owen.* Edited by W. H. Goold. Vol. 3, *Discourse on the Holy Spirit.* Edinburgh: Johnstone & Hunter, 1852.

The Oxford Dictionary of the Christian Church. Edited by F. L. Cross. London, Oxford University Press, 1961.

Packer, J. I. *A Quest for Godliness: The Puritan Vision of the Christian Life*. Wheaton, Ill.: Crossway, 1990.

Sibbes, Richard. *The Complete Works of Richard Sibbes*. Vol. 1, *The Description of Christ*. Edinburgh: James Nichol, 1862.

Smith, Henry. *Three Sermons Made by Henry Smith*. London, 1673, 1675.

Watson, Thomas. *Practical Divinity: The Lord's Prayer*. Philadelphia: Thomas Wardle, 1833.